D0978315

DİVORCED
DADS

101 ways to stay connected
with your kids

Nancy J. Wasson, Ph.D., and Lee Hefner

Adesso Press

Adesso Press
P.O. Box 489
Pinson, AL 35126

Cover design: Kathi Dunn
Editing: Robin Quinn
Book design and layout: The Roberts Group Editorial & Design Services

Publisher's Cataloging-in-Publication
(Provided by Quality Books, Inc.)

Wasson, Nancy J.
    Divorced dads: 101 ways to stay connected with your kids / by Nancy J. Wasson and Lee Hefner. — 1st ed.
    p. cm.
    Includes bibliographical references and index.
    LCCN 2002105013
    ISBN 0-9720090-0-0

    1. Divorced fathers — Family relationships. 2. Children of divorced parents—Family relationships. 3. Father and child. 4. Parenting, Part-time. I. Hefner, Lee. II. Title.

HQ756.W37 2002   306.874'2
                    QB102-200368

Attention Corporations, Universities, Colleges, and Professional Organizations: Quantity discounts are available on bulk purchases of this book for educational, gift purposes, or as premiums for increasing magazine subscriptions or renewals. Specific books or book excerpts can also be created to fit specific needs.

Visit our Web site at www.staydad.com.

Dedications

For my lovely daughter Susanna,
Who has always been an inspiration to me
— L. H.

For my beloved son John,
Who is truly a blessing in my life
— N. W.

For all divorced dads and their children,
May you experience delight in your relationships.
— N. W. & L. H.

Acknowledgments

PRODUCING THIS WORK HAS BEEN OUR FIRST ENTRY into the world of book writing and publishing. We would like to thank those individuals who have encouraged us and contributed to making this book a reality.

Dan Poynter was instrumental in teaching us the nuts and bolts of book publishing. We attended his seminar in January 2001, held in his beautiful Santa Barbara, California home overlooking the Pacific Ocean, and we came away changed forever.

At Dan's workshop, Alex Carroll gave us tremendous insight into ways to get the word out about our book. More than anyone else in the last year, his example of success has been instrumental in keeping us moving forward.

Novelist Vanessa Davis Griggs has given us hope with her positive, upbeat enthusiasm and energy. Always gracious about sharing her expertise as an author, Vanessa has been an inspirational example of what positive thinking and believing can accomplish.

When we first talked to Robin Quinn, we knew at once that she was a perfect fit to edit the book. Her background, experience, and sensitivity to the topic let us know that we had found the right person. We are grateful for Robin's expertise and assistance.

Sherry and Tony Roberts were lifesavers by their timely assistance with the book design and layout. We are deeply appreciative for their flexibility, knowledge, and dependability.

Kathi Dunn delighted us with her creative cover design. With many major authors' book-cover designs on her resume, Kathi's credentials are most impressive. She was a pleasure to work with, and we feel fortunate that she could fit us into her busy schedule.

We also want to thank our parents and children, as well as friends too numerous to name here, for being blessings in our lives. And above all, we are thankful to God for the spiritual connection that sustains us daily.

Author's Note

All individuals mentioned in examples and stories in *Divorced Dads* are composite characters drawn from our life experiences. Names and details have been changed to protect confidentiality.

Please note that we alternate between the use of male and female pronouns throughout the book. This is to avoid the awkward "him or her" phrasing. Also we primarily use the words "children" and "kids" while acknowledging that some fathers will have only one child from the marriage that ended in divorce.

Disclaimer

THIS BOOK IS DESIGNED AS A GENERAL GUIDE for noncustodial, divorced fathers, and it aims to provide tips to complement other parenting efforts. As a general guide, it is not intended to be used in place of therapy or professional support. The reader is encouraged to consult with professionals such as counselors, psychologists, family therapists, physicians, and attorneys for specific guidance. The authors are not attorneys, and this book is not intended to provide legal advice. A divorced father should consult an attorney if he thinks he may need legal advice related to his particular situation.

There will be times when courts may limit contact between a child and a father because of abuse or other reasons. Custodial mothers need to consult with an attorney when there are safety issues involved. The authors of this book in no way advocate exposing any child to unsafe, harmful, or abusive situations. *A child's safety must always take precedence over other issues and concerns.*

Although the authors have diligently worked to ensure the accuracy and completeness of the information presented, they assume no responsibility for errors, inaccuracies, omissions, or inconsistencies herein. Therefore this text should be used only as a guide and not as the ultimate authority on parenting or divorce issues. Neither the authors nor Adesso Press shall have any liability or responsibility to any person or entity with respect to any loss or damage caused, or alleged to have been caused, directly or indirectly, by the information contained in this book.

Parenting is not always easy. Divorced parents should expect to devote considerable time and effort in order to produce their desired results. The recommendations that are offered in this book are not suitable for all parents or families. Each divorce situation is unique, and no book or approach can cover all possibilities and concerns.

Contents

CHAPTER 4

CHAPTER 5

CHAPTER 6

Preface

THIS BOOK IS A GUIDE TO HELP DIVORCED DADS develop deeper emotional ties with their children and stay bonded with them. If your kids live with your ex-spouse, and you have an interest in staying connected with the children in a meaningful way now and in the years ahead, you'll want to continue reading.

Divorced Dads: 101 Ways to Stay Connected with Your Kids grew out of our mutual interest in divorce issues. For nearly two years, we had on-going discussions with each other about ways to help kids from divorced families adjust to their new circumstances. The discussions eventually led to our current focus on how challenging it is after a divorce for noncustodial fathers to maintain quality relationships with their children.

Divorced dads in particular have interested Lee for some time. Because he is a divorced father, Lee has struggled with the issues that have come with trying to maintain a meaningful parent-child relationship in the ten years since he and his wife separated. As a divorced mom, Nancy also has personal experience with many of the dynamics involved in divorce. Professionally, in her twenty-five years of clinical counseling, she has observed that noncustodial fathers typically have problems connecting with and staying close to their kids after divorce. Together, we have created the list of methods and techniques in this book. Many of these Lee has used himself; others were derived from the experiences of numerous divorced fathers who have found ways to stay connected with their children.

Use the ideas and examples you'll find in *Divorced Dads* to trigger your own creativity and imagination. They are designed to provide a starting point to get you thinking and talking about what else you might do in *your* relationship with *your* kids that could be helpful. Over time, you will come up with your own approach that works for you and the children. It's our hope that these tips will serve as a springboard to a deeper, more fulfilling relationship with your kids.

With empathy for divorced fathers everywhere, we send our book out into the world with hope and anticipation. May the ideas it contains bless your life by helping you nurture a great asset, the intimate connection you have with your children.

Nancy Wasson, Ph.D., and Lee Hefner
June 2002

Introduction

LIKE SO MANY OTHERS, are you a dad who has let his children slip away after a divorce? And are you now wondering how to get that rapport with your kids back? There are a number of possible solutions that can get you the results you want. The way to your child's heart has many conceivable paths. You don't always know which one will work. Be like a persistent ant that is determined to get into a house. First he tries to walk under the front door. If he can't get through, the ant attempts to enter via a crack by a window frame. If that still doesn't work, he finally climbs up the chimney and down into the fireplace.

This book covers many different ways to get close to your children. Even if just one works for you, it will be worth far more than the effort it will take you to read these tips. And you will enjoy its fruit for the rest of your life.

Lee's Story

"Daddy," sobbed my six-year-old daughter Susanna over the telephone, "when are you coming back home?" It wasn't the first time Susanna had asked me this question since I had left my daughter and her mother months before. And yet it still hurt me to hear Susanna ask it.

How could I tell her that I was not coming back? I asked myself this question again and again. I had not been able to bring myself to tell her the whole truth, in part because I was confused myself. Was I going back or not? Could my wife and I really reconcile our differences? I was not alone in my suffering. Millions of fathers every year agonize over the issues and problems of struggling with a difficult marriage. And many, after going through tremendous emotional turmoil, finally get divorced, just as I did.

Looking back, I can see that I have experienced many of the same emotions and dilemmas other divorcing fathers face. Anger, bitterness, and hostility were just a few of the emotions that my ex-wife and I had to deal with following our breakup. And through it all, it became very easy for me to overlook the needs of my daughter. She needed a dad to be a support for her—emotionally, socially, and financially. What she got was a father distracted by conflict with her mother and by his career.

After almost ten years of being a long-distance father to my daughter, I have learned much from my own experience. I've also gained insight from the experiences of other fathers who have worked on maintaining connections with their kids after divorce. And I have found in my own relationship with my daughter a rebirth in communication between us, resulting from my use of the principles contained in this book.

What Can You Do?

If you're a divorced dad interested in maintaining and improving your relationship with your children, this book was written for you. It is a compilation of principles and techniques that are designed for dads who are frustrated by the difficulty of maintaining good emotional links with their kids. At the same time, the fathers have all the normal feelings of love for their children. One of our goals is to help dads master a hidden treasure of opportunity by giving them the tools they need. And in reaching this goal, we hope to improve the world a little by giving children more of what they truly deserve—a loving father who is there for them when they need him the most.

Kids need their dads just as much after divorce as they did before the divorce. The fact that there is less time to spend with a father after the divorce means that every minute together becomes even more precious. Therefore it is important for you to understand what will help you create and maintain a quality relationship with your children so that you can optimize the time you that you have.

With this book, we offer the possibility of a renewed and reinvigorated link with your kids. It teaches you how to do four basic things:

1. Define what it is that you really want with and for your children.

2. Lay the groundwork with your ex-spouse and others in your children's lives so that you can connect better with your kids and give them necessary support.

3. Develop the parenting and communicating skills that will help you bond with your children.

4. Learn a number of methods and techniques to stay well-connected with your kids.

The tips contained in the following chapters will assist you during the times between visitations when your kids are with their mother, in school, or involved in a social activity. The ideas will also enrich the times when your children are visiting you or you are together on an outing.

The actions that you choose to take now in relating to and communicating with your children will affect your relationship for years to come. Even if you are dissatisfied and disheartened about your current relationship with your kids, there is always hope. There are specific things we share in this book that you can do *right now* to impact the quality of your bond with your kids. By keeping positive and by taking constructive action, you are putting yourself in the best possible place for good things to happen for you and your children.

CHAPTER 1

Decide What You Want: Develop Your Vision

What outcomes do you want in your relationship with your kids? What are your parenting goals and priorities? These are questions that can help you to identify and clarify what you wish to accomplish. It's fairly easy to state broad goals such as, "I want to be a good father" or "I want to do all I can to help my kids." However, in order to develop a game plan that will maximize your chances of success, you'll need to be more specific and precise.

In looking at how to meet your goals, it will be important to assess what your strengths are as a father. It will be essential to identify what you need to learn so that you can fill in any gaps in your parenting skills. These steps, combined with setting priorities and goals, form the basis for a successful plan of action.

Most fathers want to have the opportunity to stay closely connected with their kids. They want to do their part in helping the children grow up into happy, well-adjusted adults. Yet there are several barriers that can prevent a father from realizing these objectives. First, he may not have a clear vision or definite objectives about what he wants for his kids and the quality of his relationship with them. Second, his relationship with his ex may have deteriorated to a low point. After encountering consistent resistance from her, he may become discouraged and conclude that his children are largely inaccessible except for court-ordered visitation. Third, even during visitations, he may not know how to offer the nurturing that kids need, and he may actually do things that harm his efforts to build a loving relationship with the children.

Developing a plan for parenting will give direction to your efforts. Imagine yourself as a father with a wonderful relationship with your child. The time you spend together is special, and both of you share a satisfying bond of closeness that seems to get even better as time passes. *This outcome is possible*. The fact that you are divorced does not have to harm your bond with your child. On the contrary, some men actually improve the connection with their children after they are separated from a wife. This can be possible for you too if you first spend time developing your vision and creating a goal-oriented action plan. The tips in this chapter will show you how to do this.

Set Priorities

Get clear in your own mind about the importance of your children in your life.

What are your priorities? What is most important to you? When asked these questions, many dads immediately reply that the kids are one of their top priorities. If this is true for you, then ask yourself the following three questions:

1. Am I really connecting with my children in the way that I would like?

2. If not, then why not?

3. Am I allowing conflict with my ex-wife to get in the way?

Unfortunately dads often do not know how to establish and enjoy a more healthy and loving relationship with their kids. In fact, divorced fathers are frequently so bogged down in acrimony with their ex-partners that they fail to pay enough attention to what matters the most to them until it's too late.

As a noncustodial dad, you probably have court-ordered visitation privileges. Therefore time is precious because you have limited visitation with your children. Unless you take action, days, weeks, and months could easily slip by, and your children might grow up without the involvement from you that they need and deserve. How are you going to use the time that you *do* have to your best advantage to improve your connection with your kids? What steps are you going to take to improve your bond of trust and love so that when you and your children are not together that connection will still be strong?

Too often divorced dads feel hopeless and discouraged

in their attempts at noncustodial parenting. It is all too easy to decide to back off, stop trying, or drop out of your kids' lives. You *can* take steps to change your situation, but the change must begin with *you*. First, you have to decide what you really want for your children and for yourself. Second, you have to be willing to do whatever it takes to have a good relationship with your kids. Third, you have to take action.

CRAIG HAD ALWAYS LOVED HIS CHILDREN, *but he and his ex-wife Jenny fought continuously. She made it difficult for him to talk to his two children between visitations. Jenny had learned to adjust to life without Craig. In fact, it was easier for her to handle the kids if Craig were not even involved at all, since his phone calls to the kids disrupted their evening schedules and often left them in an agitated state. Afterwards Jenny had problems getting them to finish their homework and go to bed on time. As the strain between Craig and Jenny continued, he became increasingly frustrated that it was so difficult to connect with his children. Craig was also embarrassed that he was behind on his child support. Finally, at one point, his anger exploded. "What's the use," he thought. "She's never done me right." Then he rationalized, "Who knows if the kids are even mine. How do I know she didn't cheat on me?" Over the next few months, Craig gradually withdrew from trying to see or contact his children. He, in effect, abandoned them. The kids, in turn, grew up without knowing their father. It was sad because all of them lost. Things could have turned out much differently if Craig had only had the right tools and the resolve to use them.*

Get Clear on What Matters Most

Try this exercise. Imagine that you're standing in the middle of some railroad tracks. Far ahead of you, by the side of the tracks, you can see a gathering of people. You are surprised, as you realize that the gathering is actually a funeral. You see the podium, the flowers, the coffin. And now various people from the assembly take turns at the microphone, offering remembrances of the person who is deceased. A middle-aged woman gets up to speak. She looks familiar. You vaguely feel as if you should know her. Then, with sudden horror and shock, you realize that this woman is your own aging daughter, and the person she is eulogizing is *you*.

As she approaches the podium, you realize that you're looking into the future, and you marvel at how she now looks, so many years later. What will she say? That her parents let anger and bitterness between them get in the way of being there for her? That she was glad that you spent so much time climbing the ladder of success that she never got to see you? That even when the two of you were together, you never related to her in a way that was nurturing or encouraging of strong self-esteem and confidence?

Or will she say that you turned off the television when the two of you were together so that you could really listen to her? Will she say that you made the effort to be there for her school play? And that you did not let lack of rapport with her mother stop you from being a good parent?

You look down at the railroad track you're standing on. It's actually a timeline and where you're standing on the track represents one point in time. In back of you is your past. You see behind you your ex-spouse and all the other things that stand out in your memory. You cannot change any of that. In front of you is your future. And every tie in the track represents one day of your life. The choices you make every day during your daughter's childhood will determine the memories she takes with her to your funeral.

You get to choose which funeral scenario will take place. It's your call. You can have a child who remembers your parenting efforts and the time spent together with fond memories. Or you can have a child who recalls your lapses in effort and lack of sensitivity to her needs.

How will your child remember you? You are answering that question by the choices you are making today.

 TIP 2

State Your Goals as a Father

By defining what you want to accomplish, you establish a clear direction for you and your children.

When you were a child, did you have any positive experiences that you would like your kids to experience? Or did you have any negative experiences that you would not want your children to have to undergo? Perhaps you know of other dads who have done things for their kids that you would like to emulate. Or maybe you have observed, heard about, or read of individuals who acted out in socially unacceptable ways and whose behavior contributed to unhappy childhoods.

It will be helpful to state the particular goals that you want to accomplish concerning your kids. For example, be more specific than just saying that you want your children to experience a happy life. What do you think it would take for your kids to be happy? Do they need a good education so that they can get a satisfying job? Adequate social skills so that they can make and keep friends? Hobbies and activities that they can enjoy in their spare time? Good health? How do you want your children to turn out? What are the qualities you would like them to exhibit?

If you're not being proactive in guiding your relationship with your kids, the first step is to get clear about your goals. Once you have identified your intentions, then you can look at how to best pursue them. There can be many different ways to reach your children's hearts, even after a period when you have lost rapport with them. It can help to remember a phrase used in Alcoholics Anonymous—*Easy does it*. Go easy on yourself. Set your goals, and then take small steps at first.

4 Tips for Forming Goals

1. **Get clear on what you want**. A goal is like a road map. It helps you get where you'd like to go. Where do you want to go in your relationship with your children? Which direction do you need to take to get there?

2. **Always express your goals in positive terms instead of negative ones**. Instead of stating, "My goal is not to be late when I pick up Alicia for visitations," make your statement positive. One possibility is: "My goal is to be right on time when I pick up Alicia."

3. **Make your goal statements as specific as possible**. Instead of saying, "I want Alicia to be a good person," be more specific. State "I want Alicia to learn to be honest."

4. **Write down your goals and review them often**. The written word is powerful, and putting your desires in writing helps to clarify them and to anchor the goals in your mind. This increases the odds that you will follow through.

Assess Your Strengths

What skills and talents can you use in parenting that you already have?

Since you're looking for ways to stay connected to your kids, the first thing you will want to do is assess what your strengths are now. However, if you're feeling discouraged and disheartened about your chances for developing a closer bond with your children, you may be feeling down on yourself at the moment. As a result, you might be tempted to respond that you don't have any areas of strength.

Well, the reality is that everyone has strengths, abilities, interests, and talents that could be useful in helping kids learn and grow. You might have a great sense of humor and be able to see the funny side of most situations. Your children could benefit from learning to do that too. If patience is your long suit, your modeling of this trait can help your children learn to be less impatient. Maybe you are known for your loyalty to your friends, your personal honesty, your ability to work hard, or your commitment to excellence on the job. The example you set in these areas could make a major impact on your children's lives.

What if you have made some serious mistakes and you're still working on getting your life where you want it to be? One strength might be your willingness to be honest and open about the mistakes you have made and what you have learned from them. Of course, what you share will depend on the age and the maturity of your children. But know that a father who turns his life around and shares some of the process with his kids is giving them a real gift. It can make a profound impression on a child to see his father stop drinking too much, learn to control his anger, or start going to church on a regular basis.

If you assess your abilities, you're probably good at a number of things that your children would like to learn from you. And even if you're not the best at any one thing, as long as you enjoy what you're doing, you have something of value to share. One place to look would be your hobbies. Perhaps you like to fish or to fix things around the house. Or maybe you're skilled at using a computer and enjoy playing long-distance games on the Internet. You might be a creative chef or have artistic talents such as drawing, painting, or playing music. Some men enjoy working in their yards or gardens. Others like to spend time building things. Your children could benefit from learning to do these things too. These activities represent strengths and positive experiences that you can offer to your kids.

5 Questions to Ask Yourself to Identify Strengths

1. **What do other people think are your best qualities, abilities, or strengths?** To answer this question, think back to comments from parents, teachers, coaches, friends, employers, co-workers, or others who have known you.

2. **What interests do you have that could be shared with your children?** You might know a lot about antique cars, baseball, jazz, dinosaurs, history, or science fiction.

3. **What hobbies do you have now, or have you enjoyed earlier, that could be shared with your children?** For example, you might not currently collect anything, but as a youngster, you may have had a stamp or coin collection.

4. **What sports activities have you been involved in?** Could you do any of the following activities with your children: kayaking, canoeing, swimming, snorkeling, scuba diving, bowling, tennis, golf, martial arts, ping pong, hiking, badminton, or jogging?

5. **What skills have you developed that you could teach your children?** Can you build a birdhouse, repair a lawnmower, refinish a dresser, paint a bedroom, unstop a clogged sink, hang a picture correctly, put up a tent, or change the oil in your car?

TIP 4 | Identify Areas of Growth

You will improve as a parent only when you're willing to admit that you are not perfect.

A stable building can only be constructed on a solid foundation. Look at the foundation of your relationship with your kids and evaluate where structural weaknesses are. This effort may require a little humility, since no one likes to admit to not being very good at something. If you find cracks in your foundation, you'll need to repair them in order to give your kids the best of you.

4 Pillars of Good Parenting

There are many qualities that a father could have that make him capable of raising balanced, healthy children. Some of the most important ones are honesty, integrity, dependability, and consistency. Our definitions of these terms are:

1. **Honesty**—Saying what you do.

2. **Integrity**—Doing what you say.

3. Dependability—Doing it when you say you'll do it.

4. Consistency—Doing it with the same quality every time.

By setting an example of honesty and integrity, you act as a role model who will positively influence your kids. One of the challenges about being honest in all things is that sometimes we don't look very good when the truth is known. When this happens, you may be tempted to hide the truth so that you can protect your image. That's why being honest sometimes requires humility to admit your faults and courage to face potential criticism. Children are very good at detecting deceit, and they will usually find out if you hide the truth from them. Everything you do will show your integrity, or how well your actions reflect what you say. If you say that you love your kids, but your actions don't show it, then you're not living with integrity.

Your dependability, consistency, honesty, and integrity will influence how much your children can trust you. Make sure your kids are able to count on you. Be on time when you pick the children up or take them back home. If you say you'll do something, then do it. Your kids' sense of security will be enhanced immeasurably if they feel that you are consistently there for them and always have the same commitment to spending quality time with them.

There is no substitute
for loving action.

TIP 5 — Take Responsibility for Your Choices and Actions

If you're willing to take responsibility for your behavior, the way will be paved for positive change in all of your relationships.

One of the most powerful decisions that a dad can make is to commit to taking responsibility for the quality of his relationship with the children. We have seen fathers who were successful in maintaining strong rapport with their kids even when relations with their ex-wives were initially very stormy after the divorce. We asked them how they kept feelings of hostility and bitterness towards their former partners from getting in the way of their closeness to the children. The common response is captured in the saying, *"If it's to be, it's up to me."* These men accepted responsibility for doing whatever it took to improve the connection with their kids.

For many dads, it has become too easy to complain about the unfairness of the court system or about how their ex-wives have "done them wrong." They are reluctant to take their share of responsibility for maintaining a strong connection with their children.

It's All in Your Mind

Viktor Frankl was a Jewish psychiatrist who, during World War II, was placed in a concentration camp by the Nazis. Frankl later wrote that the main factor that helped him survive the experience was the recognition that *he alone* controlled his attitude. Even when his captors tortured him, Frankl kept his mind focused on the outcome that he wanted rather than on the experience he was going through at the time. After the war, in his classic book, *Man's Search for Meaning*, Frankl described the basic choice that people have in determining how they react to events in their lives. The essence of what Frankl said was that no matter what happens, we always have options in how we choose to respond. So even when it doesn't seem that you have any options or control, you still have a choice about something—that is, how you react and what your attitude will be.

In getting a divorce, most people go through tremendous emotional, physical, and financial stress. When we're stressed, we become hypersensitive to what we perceive as negative or critical remarks from others, especially an ex-spouse. In a nutshell, it's very easy for your former partner to push your buttons at these times. We've heard fathers in this situation say, "I try to keep my cool when I talk to her, but she makes me lose my temper." In actuality, no one else can "make" you lose your temper. That is *your* choice.

The challenge, and the opportunity, is to realize that between the stimulus of your ex's antagonizing remarks and your angry response, there's a gap in which you can make a decision. You can decide to react defensively, or you can think about your kids, take responsibility for how you act, and compose your response accordingly.

> "There were plenty of times when I wasn't the kind of father I wanted to be. The turning point for me came when I became willing to admit that I needed to change some of my beliefs and attitudes."
> — Lee Hefner

TIP
6

Commit to Action

To bond with your children, talk is fine,
but action is what counts.

After you have decided what kind of relationship you want with your kids, you must commit to taking action. Desires or wishes are meaningless without commitment to making them a reality. It's your actual behavior that your children observe and remember. You can say you love your kids, but if you fail to show up for a planned outing, the children will remember that bitter disappointment and carry it in their hearts, possibly for years to come.

There is a period of ill will between men and their former partners in many divorces. If this is the case for you, you probably have some rebuilding to do for the good of your kids. It doesn't mean you have to be friends with your ex, although this does happen for some couples. What you do want is to be allies, since it's in both your interests to cooperate. You can help your ex in various ways, such as by being supportive of your children's school progress and projects, and by backing up her efforts to discipline. And she can help you by facilitating your access and bonding to your kids.

Be ready to do whatever it takes to deepen your relationship with the children. But go slowly at first. Too many fathers try to take too much action at once when they do decide to increase contact with their kids. This causes anxiety for both the mother and the children. Why is this? If you went through an initial period after the divorce when you were less involved with your kids, maybe they learned to view you as disconnected, distant, or uncaring. Therefore don't expect that your children will immediately welcome you back with open arms. Your ex could be suspicious that you may stir things up with a flurry of activity and then disappear again. Both the kids and your ex may reason that since you were disengaged once before, you could easily revert to that behavior again. And many fathers do retreat if they don't have initial success in reestablishing a bond with their kids. You will have to be more persistent and prove yourself as you go along.

Start by taking small steps to improve your relationship with your ex and to deepen your connection with your children. Build their trust by doing what you say you'll do. Be consistent in your attempts to bridge the gap between yourself and your kids, and think long term. If you work at it and have patience, you will show that you have your priorities straight. You'll convey that you're a determined dad who knows how to back up his words with action.

4 Steps for Making a Beginning

1. **Pick a short-range goal to work on**. Start with a minor goal that is achievable in a fairly short period of time. This might be to meet your child's teachers or to send your child a funny card in the mail each week for a month.

2. **Break the goal down into even smaller steps that are measurable.** Trying to do a good job as a father is not an objective, measurable goal. Stating that you will call your child twice each week is objective and measurable. At the end of the week, you can evaluate your progress and see if you are on course.

3. **Set a timeline for the smaller steps that you have identified.** If you're going to plan a day excursion for your children's next visitation, set deadlines for researching options, sending information to your kids, talking with them about what they would like to do, and making a final decision and whatever advance arrangements are necessary.

4. **Remember to give yourself praise for the efforts you're making.** Small steps lead to bigger steps, and the important thing is to keep moving forward. Don't look back with regret about what you have missed with your kids. If you do, you will get bogged down in the past and will lose momentum. Instead, focus on the progress you are making now and the positive direction you are going in.

CHAPTER 2

Mend Fences: Create a Team Approach with Your Ex

Kids need both parents to be involved with them. Your role as a father will be much easier if you and your ex-spouse can form a team approach to co-parenting instead of having two different armed camps. You will be connected to your ex

through your children for the rest of their lives. So it is to everyone's advantage, *especially your children's*, if you can advocate for and create a cooperative approach to dealing with parenting issues.

Ideally team members put aside personal differences so that they can accomplish their overall goal. In your case, *you and your ex would make raising physically and emotionally healthy, happy, resilient children a top priority.* Some mothers might feel that they don't need the father's help, and they may wish that he would drop out and not be a part of the children's lives. Nancy has worked with cases in counseling where these same mothers have been surprised at how helpful it can be to have their ex's support. This support can be crucial when kids go through difficult stages, such as being disrespectful, disobedient, or rebellious, or when they experience academic or behavior problems at school.

Don't be discouraged if your ex is doubtful, hesitant, or resistant at first to your requests or proposed plans. Change can be threatening, and many people have a natural resistance to doing things differently. If you have been predominantly in the background of your children's lives and you want to become more actively involved, this will be a major change for your ex. She is likely to experience increased stress, anxiety, and frustration in the beginning stages of building a team approach. Yet, over time, you both can develop ways to reduce the friction and smooth out the rough spots in your interactions.

Keep in mind that team members support, encourage, and help each other. In addition, they focus their efforts and energy on achieving their common goals. Throughout this process, *put your children's welfare first,* and remember that *creating a strong team approach with your ex is a critical step to strengthening your connection to your kids.*

Check Your Thinking

Your thoughts are the ancestors of the actions you take.

Fathers who are willing to look at and question their own thinking regarding an ex-spouse and the kids can change their own future history. Lee found that by changing his own thinking, he was able to communicate more effectively with his ex. This, in turn, changed the quality of Lee's rapport with his daughter.

You may be saying to yourself, "But you just don't know my situation. You don't know my ex. Her behavior is driving me bananas. What good will it do to change *my* thinking when *she* is the problem?"

Often there is a stalemate in the relationship between ex-partners that is typified by troubled communications and angry exchanges. In this context, it's no wonder that the relationship between a father and his children suffers. But when you change the status quo with your ex-partner, you open up possibilities for better intimacy with your kids. This idea is called *the Mobile Principle*.

What Is the Mobile Principle?

All families, even when there has been a divorce, are like mobiles. A mobile is comprised of strings, rods, and things hanging down in static balance. If you touch one hanging object, it affects the overall balance of the whole mobile, and all the pieces move. Likewise, if you make any move in the relationship with your ex or the kids, they will respond. If your behavior changes enough and is consistently positive, there will be positive results, even if they take a while to manifest. Therefore, since your behavior is influenced by your thoughts, you can change the dynamics of the relationship with an ex if you change your thinking.

It will take courage to question your own thinking. However, once you do, you can reap tremendous rewards in the relationship with your children. By questioning your habitual thinking patterns, you pave the way to changing your behavior. The ancestor of every action is a thought, even though that thought may be unconscious. And if you change your own behavior positively, repeatedly, and consistently, you will inevitably increase the odds that your ex's behavior will change in a way that will be more favorable to you and your relationship with the kids.

For example, perhaps before you talk to your ex on the phone, you always think to yourself, "She's only going to criticize me and say 'no' to my request." If you think something like this, you'll probably feel anger building up even before a conversation with your ex begins. Sure enough, the scenario plays out just as you predicted, so you slam down the phone in anger. But what if you could change your thoughts about the upcoming conversation and, instead, say to yourself, "When I get angry, I close doors to finding a solution with my ex. Today when we talk, I'm going to really listen, keep my cool, and remain courteous, no matter what. I can't control what she says or does, but I can control what I say and do. And if I change my behavior, then, over time, I am opening the door for our relationship with each other to change." Now you have done your part in creating the opportunity for improved future interactions.

| TIP 8 | **Adjust Your Attitude** |

By altering the attitude you take toward your ex, you can have a positive influence on her behavior.

One of the common tendencies for divorced dads is to be stuck in bitterness toward their ex-wives. And when this feeling is mutual between the two of you, your adversarial stance creates an emotional wall that obscures the need children have to maintain a close relationship with their father. Indeed, the gulf of hostility between the two ex-partners makes it difficult for either parent to focus on what's best for their kids.

What attributes do you need to develop in order to be able to relate more harmoniously with your ex? Does your attitude help or hurt you in accomplishing the goal of staying closely connected with your children? How do you need to change or improve your attitude?

The attributes named in the box below are long-term goals. Do not be discouraged if you fall short in achieving any of them now. The aim is continuous progress. No father is a saint, and none of us is perfect. It's enough that you commit to working on improving yourself. Your ex will notice, and ultimately you and your kids will benefit.

---

6 Attributes that Support a Positive Attitude

1. **Belief** that improvement in your relationship with your ex-spouse is possible.

2. **Patience** with your ex, yourself, and the process of learning to work together as a team. It takes time to develop and refine how you and your ex will handle both routine and unexpected situations.

3. **Consistent Effort** over time with sustained motivation and energy.

4. **Accepting Responsibility** for your actions, mistakes, and shortcomings.

5. **Willingness to Persevere** in spite of discouragement and unexpected problems.

6. **Tolerance** for your ex's traits, habits, and differing viewpoints that exasperate you.

TIP 9 | Redirect Your Reactions

When you can change your reaction to the situation between you and your ex, your outcomes will be different.

Perhaps you're frustrated with the situation regarding your children. The court system may have made restrictions limiting contact, you might have a strained relationship with your ex, and you could believe that nothing will improve in the situation. Well, we believe that you *can change* the outcome of almost any situation that you're involved with. What counts is not what happens to you; it's how you *respond* to what occurs. If you take responsibility for deciding how you will respond, you can change the dynamic with your ex in a way that will set the stage for better rapport with your children.

Typically, when something happens to us, we have a habitual response. Say that your ex-wife criticizes you. What is your response? Are you defensive? Angry? Do you lash out? You could decide to change your type of response and to redirect your feelings. Instead of immediately reacting with anger, you could experiment with what it feels like to detach somewhat emotionally. In this type of response, you would take time to just observe what is happening as if you were a news reporter. Or you could focus for a while on being curious about why your ex feels and acts as she does. Both of these approaches can help to change the intensity of your emotional reactions. If you can learn to change your response to triggers that make you angry, anxious, or fearful, both you and your kids will ultimately benefit.

How to Cope with Anxiety and Fear

- **Be willing to recognize your own insecurities.** Put labels on them (for example, "I feel anxious because my ex-wife is making plans to marry her boyfriend.")

- **Feel your emotions.** These function as the indicator lights on the control panel of your consciousness. If you ignore your feelings, it could be like ignoring the flashing red oil light on your car's dashboard.

- **Identify what emotion you're feeling.** If it's a negative emotion, chances are that fear in some form is at the basis of it. However, realize that fear is often unfounded. Most of the time, we're afraid of things that will never happen.

- **Give yourself an affirmation that contradicts the fear**, such as "Love always finds a way," "With God's help, I can cope with whatever happens," or "God helps those who help themselves, so I'll just keep on doing my part the best I can."

- **Repeat the Serenity Prayer often:** "God, grant me the *serenity* to accept what I cannot change, the *courage* to change the things I can, and the *wisdom* to know the difference."

Experiment with the above affirmations and prayers, or create your own. Repeat them over and over. As you do, visualize things working out in a positive way.

Work on Becoming Allies

*If you can create a cordial rapport with
your ex, your kids will thank you.*

Children always suffer emotionally when their divorced
parents treat each other with disrespect and rudeness. Even
if there are unresolved issues that still hurt and anger you,
be big-spirited enough to be courteous and gracious during your telephone and in-person contacts with your ex-
spouse. If you're having difficulty in letting go of the resentment, bitterness, and hostility, find a good therapist to
help you. *Your kids will know if you're seething with anger
toward their mother, even if you do not express your feelings
verbally. This will harm your relationship with them.*

Accomplishing your goal of staying connected with your
kids will be much easier to do if you and your ex have a
smooth, cordial relationship that facilitates good communication and a team approach to co-parenting. Why spend
time and energy holding onto anger and negativity towards
your ex when you could be putting effort into improving
the relationship with your kids? Why not put the past behind you and help your children by taking steps to move
on to a more positive present and future?

It just makes good sense to do what you can to gain the
cooperation and assistance of your ex in matters pertain-
ing to the kids. You're going to need her help in providing
you with current information about your children and in
supporting your efforts to stay deeply connected to them.
*So put your own personal feelings aside, use your best manners
and relationship skills, and make doing what's best for your kids
the top priority.*

5 Tips for Mending Fences with Your Ex

1. **Begin talking with your ex about creating a team approach to parenting** that would be beneficial to your kids as well as helpful for her and yourself.

2. **Take responsibility for your part in what happened** in your marriage and divorce, as well as for what has occurred since then. Avoid blaming your ex.

3. **Apologize for your mistakes, hurtful actions, and shortcomings, and mean it.**

4. **Do whatever you have to do to start the process of releasing resentments and forgiving your ex.** See a therapist, talk to your minister, pray or meditate daily.

5. **Tell your ex that you're working on changing yourself and that you want to be a better parent.** Ask for her help and suggestions. Then listen to what she has to say and thank her.

Offer to Help Your Ex When You Can

If you are helpful to your ex-spouse, she may be more willing to be supportive of your efforts to stay connected to the kids.

There are times when you may need to help your ex to purchase or to learn how to use certain equipment that will assist you in staying in touch with your children. For example, if you want to be able to email the kids, your ex-spouse may need help in figuring out how to set up her computer. She might want your emails to be received while inappropriate messages from some other sources are blocked. Share your knowledge of the options available with her if you know how this can be done, or offer to make telephone calls to research possible solutions.

If you want your ex to take pictures of the kids with a digital camera and to send them to you by email, you may need to provide the equipment and instructions on how to do so. If your kids are old enough to take the pictures themselves, depending on their ages, your ex would still need to supervise their use of the camera and the transmission of the pictures to you. *Express appreciation for your ex's willingness to "go the extra mile."* Even relatively simple actions take time and energy, and the reality is that there are often hidden snags or time-consuming glitches that occur.

Some divorced dads are reluctant to do anything extra to help their former mates, and they may have made comments at the time of divorce about "never lifting a finger to help her again." In their resentment, these dads are forgetting that their ex-wives are handling many routine details of everyday life involving the children that the men never have to worry about. These fathers are also forgetting that there will be times when they will want their ex-wives to be flexible and willing to do extra things to help them keep in close touch with their kids.

Lee often talks about the concept of making plenty of "goodwill" deposits in the relationship bank. That way, when you need to ask for extra understanding or patience from another person, you have enough goodwill accumulated in the account to cover the request. *Be supportive of your ex by sharing knowledge and resources, offering to help gather information or explore possible options, and thanking her for assistance in helping you to develop a variety of ways to stay connected to your kids.*

4 Questions to Ask Yourself

1. Would you deprive your ex of something just to get personal satisfaction, even though providing it would help your kids?

2. Do you want your children to remember you as petty, mean-spirited, and bitter, or to remember you as generous, kind-hearted, and compassionate?

3. Do you always insist that everything in your relationships with others has to be absolutely fair, not ever wanting to give more than what you feel is your fair share and continually keeping score?

4. Is it time to let the past go and to become the kind of father that your kids will respect, admire, and love? If not now, when will you do this?

| TIP 12 | **Be Supportive of Your Ex's Parenting Efforts** |

Taking steps to be supportive of your ex-spouse is part of the groundwork you need to do to help your children, to create goodwill, and to increase the chances that your efforts to stay connected with your kids will succeed.

It's only natural and to be expected that you and your ex-spouse will disagree about parenting issues at times. If you have put time and effort into establishing a cordial relationship with your ex, then you will have a better chance of being able to express your concerns and opinions when this happens. Don't criticize your ex-wife in conversations with your kids, call her names, put the ex down, or make fun of her. *Remember that your children are a combination of both you and their mother*. Criticizing your ex is the same as putting down that part of your kids that they inherited from their mother, and this can affect your children's self-esteem.

Make a resolution with your ex to be supportive of each other in front of the kids and to settle any differences privately. This will keep your children from feeling "caught in the middle" and developing anger toward you for putting them in that position. Making this resolution means that it's not fair to use your children to deliver messages to your ex-wife, such as "Tell your mother that I'm going to pick you up on Saturday morning instead of Friday evening." It's also not fair to complain to your kids if you think the divorce financial settlement was a raw deal for you. Nancy has known fathers who tell their kids, "If I didn't have to give your mom so much money each month, I'd be able to buy you that PlayStation." It is *never* fair to put kids in the middle of any of your issues with your ex.

Even if your ex does not keep her part of the agreement, be sure that you do. You cannot control what she chooses to do, but you can control *your actions*. Take the high road and show respect for your children by refraining from berating their mother. If you slip and say something unflattering about your ex, apologize to the kids and tell them that you're working on changing that behavior.

When you talk privately with your ex-spouse to iron out your differences, be respectful of her opinions and viewpoints. Remember that two individuals can disagree and still have a courteous conversation. Conflict resolution involves listening to the other person and trying to understand where that person is coming from. It also involves the ability to generate creative options and to compromise. By doing this, you're modeling for your kids how to resolve differences in a way that respects both individuals and leads to successful solutions. This is a very valuable skill for them to learn, and you are teaching them with every word you say and every action you take.

How to Prepare for Talks about Emotional Issues

1. **Take time to center yourself emotionally by sitting quietly for a few minutes.** You might take deep belly breaths and count your out-breaths to keep yourself focused in the present moment, or you might meditate or pray during this time.

2. **Notice any negative "chatter" in your mind and replace it with a positive statement**, such as "Each time I really focus on listening intently to my ex instead of jumping in to criticize, I'm improving our working relationship." Or "I know that we can resolve this problem about how to handle Brian's weekend baseball practice."

3. **Expect to be able to get along, talk respectfully and courteously to each other, and find creative solutions to problems.** We influence what happens in interactions with others by our expectations about what we *think* will happen. In other words, you often get what you expect.

4. **Suspend judgment and criticism so that you're prepared to really hear your ex.** Resolve to listen deeply so that you can understand the fears and concerns that are layered beneath her surface words. When you can identify and understand her deeper concerns, you're more likely to find an acceptable solution.

| TIP 13 | **Recognize Your Ex's New Spouse or Partner** |

Your kids will ultimately benefit if you establish good relations with an ex's new partner.

If your ex-spouse has remarried or is in a committed relationship, *go out of your way to initiate courteous, nonthreatening interactions with her new husband or partner.* This is usually extremely challenging to do, as many divorced dads experience jealousy or resentment when confronted with an ex's new romantic choice. These feelings can surface even when you were the one who initiated the divorce.

You may find that rejection and anger are easily aroused when you see your ex with another man or hear the new partner answer the phone when you call your kids. The new man in your ex's life may have traits and characteristics that irritate you immensely, and he might take advantage of every opportunity to try to push your buttons and to deliberately annoy you. The new husband or boyfriend may engage in a series of on-going attempts to show you how much power he has over your ex-spouse, your kids, and, consequently, over you.

If you react with anger, retaliation, or a jousting for control, you're setting yourself up to lose. The reality is that the new husband or partner's opinions and wishes carry weight with your ex, whether you like it or not. And he's there every day interacting with your children, influencing the household emotional climate, and probably giving input into the decisions your ex makes that affect the kids, whether you agree or not.

You don't have to like the new partner on the scene, although some divorced dads have been surprised to find that they *do* like their ex's new choice. Even if you never grow to like him, there's nothing to be gained by antagonizing this person or engaging in power games. The most helpful approach is to be courteous and to *remain focused on your goals of building a team approach with your ex and staying connected to your kids.*

5 Guidelines for Dealing with the New Man in Your Ex's Life

1. If your ex's new husband or partner is spending time with your kids in a meaningful way or is being helpful to them, tell him how much you appreciate what he is doing.

2. Thank him whenever you have the opportunity and try to create an expanded team approach that includes him as a support person.

3. Go out of your way to give the new husband or partner recognition and appreciation, and guard against being drawn into power struggles.

4. Resist the temptation to say anything negative about him to your kids because this will only make the children feel the need to choose sides. This added pressure will create unhealthy stress for your kids.

5. Treat the new husband or partner the way you would want to be treated if you were in his shoes. Even if he does not reciprocate, your kids will appreciate and benefit from your approach.

Be Sensitive If You Have a New Mate

Help the children and your new partner get used to each other.

If you have a new spouse or live-in partner, you'll need to be sensitive to the various dynamics that can affect your relationship with an ex-wife and the kids. Anytime a new person joins an extended family, everyone else in the group has to adjust. When this happens, the change is seldom comfortable and it's easy for people to feel threatened. You, your ex-wife, her new spouse or partner, your new spouse or partner, and your kids comprise an extended family group, even though divorce has occurred.

If you're planning to marry or to live with a partner, you need to tell your ex-wife before the event happens. That way, your former spouse and you can decide together how to prepare your children for the upcoming change. Also, your ex-wife will want to have some time to adjust to the news before the kids are told. Even if she was the one who initiated the divorce, your ex is likely to have some conflicting feelings to deal with when you tell her of your plans. *This is normal.* Be sensitive and resist any urges to "rub" the news in, with such comments as "What a great person I am with now" or "I feel so much happier now than when I was married to you." Keep the focus on what's best for your children and on maintaining a team approach to parenting with your ex-wife.

Perhaps you've already remarried or have a live-in partner at this point. If that's the case, then hopefully by now you have been encouraging your new mate to work on developing a civil, courteous relationship with your ex-wife when they talk on the phone or see each other. Many men avoid this matter and don't want to be involved in what happens between the ex and the new partner. It's not fair to your children to do this. They deserve as conflict-free an environment as possible, whether they're with their mother or you. If emotions are seething between their mother and your new mate, the kids will be negatively affected. If you have a quality relationship with your new partner, then you'll be able to share how important it is to you for everyone to get along. Tell this partner how much positive efforts on her part will mean to you. You'll also want to share the strategy of focusing on your own reactions and the decision to take the "high road."

While some ex-wives have a difficult time accepting an ex-husband's new mate, others find that they like the new woman. Sometimes the two women become friends. In other cases, they're not close friends, but the ex-wife appreciates what the new mate is doing to help the children. Nancy has known of cases where an ex-wife has even offered to baby-sit for a new child born to the ex-husband and his new partner. These ex-wives recognized that their children loved the new baby and wanted to spend more time with the child. So *anything is possible. Just do your part. At the same time encourage your mate to do her part* to try to keep the relationship with your ex on an even keel. The winners, if you can do this, will be your kids.

Suggestions for Helping Kids Adjust

Be patient with your children. Sometimes it takes a while for kids to warm up to a father's new wife or partner. They may be reluctant to visit the two of you at first. If their mother is bitter about the turn of events, they may have heard some unflattering remarks about your new mate and already be biased against her. The children may wonder if she's going to attempt to take the place of their mother or to try to discipline them. If your new partner has children of her own, then your kids may be jealous of the time you spend with your mate's kids. Some ex-wives tell the kids that their father has chosen a new family, and this means that he no longer loves the children from his first marriage as much as he did.

So give your kids time to adjust to the changes in your life that affect their visitation with you. Don't expect everyone to love or even like each other immediately. What you *can* expect and *insist* on is that everyone is polite, respectful, and courteous to each other. That is the goal at first. Then, over time, as everyone gets to know each other better and has the opportunity to share fun experiences, they may discover that they like each other. But that cannot be forced. It has to happen on its own timetable.

During each visit, plan some time or activity that you can do by yourself with your children so you do not lose that special one-to-one connection. Kids like to have some time when they have their father's undivided attention. This is especially important if your new mate has children who live with you and are also competing for your time. Assure your children that you still love them and that your feelings for them have not changed.

CHAPTER 3

Request Support: Involve Others

Y ou'll need the support of others to help you stay informed
about what's happening in your
kids' lives. In particular, issues like
their health, school performance,
behavior, extracurricular activities, and
social skills are areas of concern that you
should know about. That way, you'll know the areas where
your children need help. Being informed, you'll be in a
better position to provide the support they need when they
need it.

People who can help you keep abreast of what's happening in your children's lives include the kids themselves
as well as virtually anyone else who sees them on a consistent basis. Naturally, many of these people will not
volunteer information unless you ask. Therefore, learn how

to ask for feedback about your kids. Remember the five Ws—who, what, where, when, and why, and also add how. These words are the beginning of open-ended questions that you can ask others about what they have observed in your children.

Sample questions that you might ask are:

- "How is Johnny doing in school?"

- "Who are his friends?"

- "Where does Rebecca go after school?"

- "What are her study habits?"

- "When does he have problems sleeping?"

- "Why did she make a D in history?"

Take the initiative and be proactive in requesting the information that you'll need in order to be supportive of your children. Do this even if it's difficult for you to ask for help. Ask anyway.

| TIP 15 | ## Set Up Channels of Communication |

If you establish contact with your children's mentors, it will be easier to keep abreast of the important events in their lives.

It's easy to lose track of what's happening in your kids' lives when you're not there every day. You have to make a special effort to collect relevant information from all the appropriate sources so that you will know what challenges the children are facing. These sources can include your ex-spouse, teachers, principals, school counselors, therapists, physicians, coaches, dance or music instructors, parents of your kids' friends, and relatives.

In the past, many fathers only knew how their children were doing based on what an ex-wife shared with them. Nowadays it is customary for noncustodial parents to have the legal right to information concerning their kids, such as school progress, medical updates, or counseling issues. However a father has to want to be involved to this extent and needs to be motivated to put forth the effort. It might be easier to just let all information about your children be funneled through your ex-spouse, but you may not have the complete picture unless you're more involved.

ROGER WAS SHOCKED *when his ex-wife called him to say that their twelve-year-old son, George, had been apprehended in a store for shoplifting a music CD. Roger asked to speak to his son and then queried him about why the attempted theft had occurred. George replied, "I don't know." Roger slowly realized that there was a lot that he had not kept up with about George, who had been angry since the divorce of his parents. After consulting with a school counselor at George's school, Roger decided to meet with a counseling therapist. Aided by input from this therapist, Roger realized that he had not been giving George the attention that his son deserved. With his ex-wife's cooperation, Roger scheduled several counseling sessions for George and himself to work on their relationship. Roger then decided that he should be taking a more active role in his son's life. After classes started in the new school year, Roger began calling on school nights to ask George questions about the current homework assignments and to encourage his son. He got to know George's teachers, his baseball coach, and the band director, all of which he had never taken the time to do before. Armed with up-to-date information, Roger was able to offer encouragement and helpful support to George.*

| TIP 16 | **Get Input from Your Ex** |

Enlist the help of your ex to keep informed about your kids' behavior and progress.

Since you're not with your children every day, you need current information from your ex-wife to know how your kids are doing at home and at school. This input will be important even if you have developed connections with others who are sharing their observations about the children.

For example, if you have requested that the school send you copies of the children's report cards each grading period, you will still want to know immediately about a poor daily grade on a test or a discipline problem at school. You also need to know immediately about significant discipline problems at home or in the neighborhood. That way, you can talk with your ex-wife about how to handle the situation, and you can back up her efforts to administer rewards and consequences for a child's behavior. This further solidifies the sense of teamwork you are striving for with your ex-spouse in raising your kids. By having current information, you can frame helpful responses and encourage your kids to do better.

It can make a dramatic difference when a father is actively involved in the ongoing issues in the children's lives. Even when peer pressure increases in the teen years, kids will usually still listen to a concerned father. Children typically long for their dad's approval and will put effort into obtaining it from a father they respect and love. You may feel a twinge of satisfaction if your ex-spouse is having difficulty with discipline, especially if you're still angry about the divorce. However this is not in your kids' best interest. Make it clear to a child that you're very displeased when he is disrespectful to his mother, to his teacher, or to any other adult. Show that you're supportive of your ex-spouse and express appreciation to her for sharing information with you about your children.

7 Areas to Keep Track Of

Ask your ex-spouse to keep you currently informed about the following areas:

1. Health problems or concerns

2. School grades and behavior

3. Special school programs, field trips, or functions

4. Home-discipline problems and issues

5. Other activities such as sports, music, dance, karate, and church

6. Emotional concerns

7. Social skills and social events

TIP
17

Obtain Recordings of Special Events

*Video and audio tapes of special events
your children participate in will help you
appreciate important milestones.*

Ask your kids' mother if she would be willing to make audio or video tapes of any special school programs, choir or
band performances, musical recitals, or other special events
that a child participates in. If she's not able to do so, perhaps your ex will know another parent who may be able to
help out. Offer to provide the tapes and to pay for the
postage, if necessary.

Doing this will provide you with some insights regarding the various experiences your kids are having when you
can't be there in person. It also helps you to feel more a
part of their lives. After you watch the video or listen to
the audio tape, then you can compliment a child on spe-
cifics of her performance and tell your daughter what a
good job she did.

When your children know you're using every available
means to stay connected and to keep up with what's happening in their lives, they receive a message from you of
love and caring. These are basic ingredients involved in
building a rapport that will last a lifetime.

Always remember to say an appreciative "thank you" to
your ex for making these opportunities possible.

JOHN USED TO ASK HIS SON MIKE *to tell him about
events that were happening at school. Mike would
usually answer in just a sentence or two, such as "I was in a band
concert last night." Mike never provided many details about his
experiences, and his dad felt frustrated about not knowing more.*

One evening, after finding out that Mike had been in a school play the day before, John asked his ex-wife for more details. During their conversation, John found out that one of the parents at Mike's school had made a video tape of the play. At John's request, his ex-wife called the other parent and made arrangements to obtain a copy, which she mailed to John. After John watched the video and saw his son play the main role in the play, he called Mike and complimented him on his performance. This meant a lot to Mike and afterwards John called to thank his ex-wife. John asked her if she might be willing to help him stay more connected to Mike by providing appropriate recordings in the future whenever possible, and his ex-wife said she would.

TIP 18	**Ask Your Kids How They Prefer to Stay Connected with You**

By getting feedback from your children, you'll be in a position to improve your rapport with them.

You need suggestions from your kids regarding how you can bond with them, because only the children know what they like the most. A basic rule of building rapport with a child is to get into that child's mindset or world. To do this, first carefully listen to and understand the wishes of the child, and then satisfy those wishes if you can.

When your children are visiting you, take some time to talk about any ideas your kids have about how you can stay in closer contact and feel more connected between visits. Develop a "How to Stay Connected" list together by writing down ideas on a piece of paper and choosing the best ones. If a child says, "I don't know" when you ask his opinion, don't be discouraged. "I don't know" is one of the most common answers many kids give their parents. Go ahead and mention any ideas you have had and ask the child how he feels about them. If he says, "That would be okay," then try the idea out and ask the child later how it was for him.

You want to keep the methods that work for you and your kids, while discarding those that are not helpful. As children get older, it's usual for them to want to make some changes, so be flexible. A child who once enjoyed twice-a-week phone calls from his dad may no longer want to talk on school nights once he's a teenager involved in numerous social phone calls each evening. He may prefer to email his dad during the week and have a phone conversation on Sunday afternoons. Be sensitive to your children's wishes and changing preferences.

JOHNNY PLAYED SECOND BASE *for his Little League baseball team. This was his first year to play, and his dad Jason, who lived in another state, had never been to one of Johnny's games. To Johnny, baseball was one of the most important things in life. Soon after the baseball season started, Jason, in one of his weekly telephone calls, asked Johnny how he wanted them to spend time together. Johnny said, "I want you to come to one of my games." When he heard this, Jason decided to take a day off from work and go to a game that very week. And to show Johnny that his dad was in tune with him, Jason brought Johnny a brand-new baseball glove. It was a truly special gift to Johnny.*

Encourage Extended Family Communication

Your kids will benefit if members of your immediate and extended family stay in touch with them.

Encourage your brothers, sisters, parents, aunts, uncles, nephews, nieces, cousins, and grandparents to stay in close contact with your children. This will benefit your kids greatly and will help to fortify their link to you. Close family ties to your immediate and extended family will provide your children with a sense of interconnecting family support.

When members of your immediate or extended family send you letters, emails, or photographs, you can forward them to your kids so that they will feel connected to everyone. That way, the children will also have the addresses of everyone. Make sure the kids have the telephone numbers too in case there's an opportunity to call. You could give the children an address book with important family members' addresses (regular and email) and telephone numbers in it. If any of the family members are a long-distance call away, give the children a calling card and show them how to use it. Also, your family would probably appreciate your passing along to them any important information about your kids so that they can stay current about their lives.

HAROLD'S TWO SISTERS LIVE IN NEW YORK *and he resides in Denver. Harold's teenaged daughter Maria is in Alaska with her mother but he manages to bring her down to visit at least once and sometimes twice a year. What really makes her visits even better is that Harold's two sisters make a special effort, and go to some expense, to fly to Denver to see Maria, if only for a weekend. They have done this for a number of years, and Harold knows that this makes Maria feel loved and valued. Between visits, he makes a special point to pass on family news to her during their phone calls and email communications. As a result, Maria has a close relationship with Harold's two sisters and a strong connection to his family.*

CHAPTER 4

Upgrade Your Parenting Skills: Connect More Deeply

Parenting leadership is about defining the direction you want your kids to grow in. As a father, you have the unique opportunity and responsibility of providing a guiding light to your children. Probably no other male figure in your children's lives will play as important a role as you do. This makes it very important for you to lead by setting an example that you would be proud to have your kids imitate. The process of guiding your children in the direction you choose is your chance to share part of yourself, your character, and your beliefs with the children.

You are your child's leader by virtue of the example you set, which reflects your personal traits such as honesty, integrity, perseverance, and courage. These qualities are defining elements of your character. They're the characteristics that make you unique in your parenting style, temperament, and attitude. These traits are also the personal attributes that your children will tend to unconsciously emulate. Children behave like their parents to the extent that they absorb the parents' example. You will notice that as you spend time with your child, he will copy you in some way. That is why it's important to consistently model the type of behavior that you would want your child to copy.

The most important element that you can add to the dynamic equation of your relationship with a child is *yourself*—your attitudes, beliefs, and conduct.

TIP 20 | Be Emotionally Available

Our culture teaches men to be emotionally detached, but emotional connection is what builds strong relationships.

The common perception in our society is that men are mostly logical, while women are the emotional ones. From early childhood, boys are taught to squelch many of their feelings. They learn to disavow tender emotions like love and compassion, while recognizing only feelings like anger or rage. It's our belief that this teaching has done a huge disservice to men, distorting their innate human nature. This social norm is harmful to a man's right to be fully expressive and emotionally healthy. We have found that relationships deepen and thrive when individuals can express positive feelings toward each other.

Under certain circumstances, both genders are emotional. Furthermore, emotions can be powerful tools to help us know ourselves better and to connect at a deep level with others. Men who deny the tender side of human experiences rob themselves of much of life's richness. If you learn to tap into the power of your emotions and use them in helpful and constructive ways, you can develop a relationship with your child that would not have been possible otherwise.

You may have lost your marriage but you don't have to lose your kids. Work on building rapport with them. Practice good listening skills and go easy on the criticism. Be supportive of what your children are trying to do, whether it's playing sports, working on school assignments, or developing their social skills. Be emotionally responsive and available to them.

RAY FELT DUPED BY HIS WIFE *during their marriage. She had an affair when Ray was away on business, and even two years after their divorce, he still harbored anger and resentment toward her because of it. Ray eventually entered counseling, and he began to look closely at his own behavior in the marriage. He soon discovered some uncomfortable facts about himself that had contributed to his wife's actions. Ray finally realized that he had been emotionally unavailable to his wife and kids by choosing to work too much. And even when Ray had been at home, he had watched television instead of paying attention to his family. Ray had justified this by saying that after working all day, he didn't feel like talking and needed to relax. This man ultimately realized that he might have been able to save his marriage by spending more quality time with the family, listening to his wife and kids, talking with them, and showing his family more of the positive emotions that he had not often expressed. Ray began making changes, and his relationship with his ex-wife and their children improved.*

Refine Your Sense of Humor

You will be more effective as a parent if you can laugh at yourself.

To give your child a sense of grounding and security, you need to be relaxed and confident. Instead, many fathers find themselves uptight over conflicts with their ex-wives and frantic to make every moment count when they're with the children. One thing that can relax you and diminish the intensity of your negative feelings is laughter. If you can find something funny in the frustrating situations you find yourself in with your kids, you can reduce your irritation and frustration. Laughter creates bonding, and people who laugh together generally feel closer to each other afterwards.

Being able to laugh at yourself can also be therapeutic. If you get to that point, it means that you don't take yourself so seriously. This can help to reduce stress, and it lets you focus your energy on solutions instead of self-criticism. It's important to make a distinction between taking what we do seriously and viewing ourselves too seriously.

DURING A VISITATION, NORM TOOK HIS SON *Tommy, along with some of the boy's friends, to a beautiful small river in a wilderness area of their state. At one point, Norm accidentally slid down a mud bank and got totally drenched. His first reaction was to feel foolish and self-conscious. But as Norm lay there in the mud, he suddenly got tickled about the situation and started to laugh. Immediately everyone else laughed, too. "I'm the Mud Monster!" Norm shouted, as he scrambled back up the bank. Still laughing, the kids ran to get out of his way. Tommy took a photo of the "Mud Monster" with Norm's camera. In the picture, Norm, still covered with mud, is clowning around with Tommy's friends. The experience provided a funny incident that Norm and his son still talk about when they visit together. And the photo that Tommy took still provokes smiles and laughter.*

Use Humor to Become Closer to Your Kids

- Record funny moments that happen when you're with your children. Capture the action in photos, movies, or sound recordings and make these memories available to your kids when they come to visit you.

- Send copies of the pictures, movies, or recordings to your children. The images and sounds will provide anchors to your kids that will remind them of happy and funny times and preserve those feelings of closeness and laughter.

TIP 22 | Work on Kindness

If you go easy on yourself, your ex, and your child, you will all be happier.

How do you define "kindness"? It means *being compassionate, caring, and tolerant.* When a child is less than perfect and makes mistakes, what do you do? How do you treat the youngster? If a child strikes out during a softball game, are you overly upset? Do you say things when you're mad that you later regret? Children can relax enough to learn from their errors and to improve when they are freed from the burden of having to do things perfectly. *Encouragement* paves the way for improvement, while harsh criticism can harm an otherwise close relationship.

Your kids will not care what you know until they know that you care. Do you yell and criticize without even listening to what they have to say? Is your tone of voice mocking or sarcastic? Even when you have to discipline your children, can they tell by your attitude and actions that you care about them and their welfare? Practicing kindness does not mean letting your kids run wild. The kindest action can be to assign consistent, appropriate consequences for misbehavior, but still communicate caring and concern for your children and their long-range potential.

Often people who were abused as children in turn abuse *their* kids. It's a cycle that repeats itself, generation after generation. By being aware of what you're doing, you have the opportunity to break this cycle. You can learn to be kind but firm and still enforce rules without being abusive or harsh. Your kids will love and respect you for it.

STEVE LEARNED TO HAVE COMPASSION *for himself when he made mistakes. And by extension, Steve's own suffering, that was brought on by the mistakes, gave him compassion for his daughter Lani. Compassion as a parent is about having mercy on a child when it might be easy to lose your temper and call her a bad name or put the child down in some way. The most important person Steve extends compassion to is his daughter. Steve encourages her to do better the next time she messes up. Meanwhile Steve cringes when he sees fathers who berate their children, thinking that they're helping to motivate them. The reality for most kids is that scorn, verbal lashings, and ridicule from their dad is nothing less than abuse. It creates scars that a child carries into adulthood.*

TIP 23 — Reframe Failure as Learning

Failure is not failure if you and your kids learn from it.

One of the barriers to a child's success is the belief that the child is a failure if she can't do something well the first time she tries, such as roller blading or diving. It's amazing how many kids will give up if they don't experience immediate success. Another barrier is the belief that the child is a failure if she can't do something as well as some of the other kids her age. This attitude will cause her to back away from trying new things.

Reframe what your children are calling failure and, instead, talk about the value of *learning experiences*. Fear of failure is the enemy of accomplishment. Every attempt to do something results in new feedback information that we can learn from. Teach your kids that it's all right to struggle with difficult tasks before they become good at doing them. Praise their efforts and persistence instead of looking for perfection. Practice makes perfect, and practice is the forerunner of skill. Try to teach that failure is always an opportunity to learn.

On Pride and Embarrassment

These two emotions are present for many dads when their children perform in public.

- **Fathers see their kids as reflections of themselves.** If a child performs badly, many dads will think, "People are judging me." They may feel that the performance reflects poorly on the quality of their parenting skills. If you're watching a child perform at a recital, in a play, or on the sports field and he is not doing well, be aware that your ego is getting involved. You're either seeing your child as an extension of yourself or you're making a judgment about your parenting skills. Either way, you're setting yourself up for an overreaction to the situation because of your embarrassment. This overreaction will not be healthy for the child.

- **Pride in your kids should be expressed whenever there is a good reason.** However praise for trivial reasons will seem phony and will not be effective. Well-deserved compliments, on the other hand, will be much appreciated by your kids. Praise can encourage them to continue the behavior that earned the good recognition and can become a self-reinforcing upward spiral. Recognize when your kids do something well, and they will be more likely to do it again, keeping the positive cycle going.

- **When a child does poorly, makes mistakes, or fails at something, be gentle in your response.** Remember that you hold the child's ego, self-esteem, and self-image in your hands. Remind yourself that you love the child and want the best for her. Do not believe for one minute that the best way to get the child to change her behavior is to harshly criticize, embarrass, or humiliate her. This will only have long-term negative effects in your relationship, and it will make her feel that she is not supported, helped, or loved by you. See this as your opportunity to practice healthy fathering in a way that will enhance your relationship with the child.

TIP 24 | Reveal Yourself

Showing your child the real you will increase the authenticity of your rapport.

Revealing yourself is the same as "being yourself" when you're around your kids. This doesn't mean that you have to explain all the details of your life. There will be issues that are not appropriate to share, like if you and your new wife or girlfriend are having problems. Similarly, if you are experiencing stress at work, you don't have to share the technical details. But you can say something general and express your genuine feelings about it. You might remark, "I'm really having to work a lot this month, and I'm frustrated because of it." Or, contrarily, you may be happy over some recognition at work that you received and decide to share some of the details with your children. Above all, share any positive feelings you have for your children. Otherwise, they may never know the true depth of your feelings. The more you show of the real you, especially your feelings, the more the kids will have a chance to know and love you.

SANDI AND HER DAD WILLIAM *were on their way to see a movie during one of her visits with him. They were talking about boys and dating, since she had confided to William that she liked a boy at school. William was struggling to provide her with some words of wisdom regarding relationships. However he felt inadequate, since his own marriage to her mother had not worked out. Suddenly, William felt an urge to open up to Sandi about his marriage to her mother. "You know," he began, "I have a lot of respect for your mom, but I think that it was a mistake for us to get married. We were just not right for each other. The good thing about it, though, was that I got a beautiful daughter." William squeezed Sandi's hand as he said the last sentence. Her smile let him know that they had connected on a deep level.*

Get Real with Your Kids
by Sharing Similar Experiences

● **It's beneficial for children to see their dad struggle to learn how to do something new.** That's why sharing an experience that is new for everyone can be important for your kids. Learning to kayak or roller blade or sail might bring everyone to the common denominator of "beginner." This will allow your kids to see a different part of you, an aspect that is often not as easily exposed in routine activities.

● **Share stories about your life that reveal ups and downs.** That way, your kids will be able to put their own challenges in context. Often, children tend to think that their own problems are unique to them, when in reality, everyone tends to experience many of the same challenges.

Practice Good Listening Skills

TIP 25

One of the most important things you will ever do with your children is to really listen to them.

If you really hear your kids, they will open up to you. Good listening is more than just understanding the words they say. It's also about picking up on body language and tone of voice. It's about feeling their emotions and hearing the feelings that are underneath the actual words they use. For many fathers, one of the biggest challenges is to develop the skill of letting a child vent without trying to fix anything. Fathers are used to fixing things, giving advice, and solving problems, so you may have to retrain yourself to listen without prematurely jumping in with the "perfect solution."

5 Tips for Good Listening

1. **Practice good listening habits.** Stop what you're doing, if at all possible, and give the child your undivided attention. If you're watching television, turn off the TV. It is best to sit down together where you'll be undisturbed for a period of time.

2. **Make good eye-contact and focus on what the child is saying.** Instead of thinking ahead to what you will say in return, just concentrate on really hearing the words, meanings, and emotions the child is trying to convey to you. Ask for clarification if you do not follow what he is saying.

3. **Develop reflexive habits in listening,** like mirroring back statements to verify that you understand what the child has said. You might say, "It sounds like you are really frustrated and discouraged."

4. **Learn how to really listen to your kids without cutting them off.** When you are talking, you cannot listen. You will learn more by holding your tongue than by trying to fix something before you really know what the problem is. Sometimes if you let a child talk as much as he wants, he will resolve the issue himself in his own mind without you having to do anything. Your most powerful tool is to listen with an open attitude.

5. **It's important to make a child feel heard.** All too often, if a child has a complaint about her father, he will rush to defend himself, to counterattack, or to otherwise evade responsibility. Why do fathers do this? It's mainly because they fear appearing weak or inadequate. By letting a child say her piece, you're not necessarily accepting blame or agreeing to anything. You are simply giving the child space to unload emotion and to make a point.

TIP 26 | Encourage Your Children

By teaching your kids to focus on their potential and to minimize their limitations, you are helping them to be all they are capable of being.

Support your kids' positive traits and abilities. Help the children to see how they can use their talents in the real world, for personal satisfaction as well as for a possible career in the future. That way, your kids will be motivated to become really good at what they like to do.

For example, if you have a son who likes to draw, be quick to encourage him to continue. Point out the opportunities and careers in which his talents could be used. He could be a graphic artist working in the advertising field, or his interest might lead to technical design, drafting, or architecture. If your son loves sports, let him know that besides being an athlete, he could also be an announcer, a trainer, a sports physician, or a team manager.

Encourage your kids to do all they can to develop their talents, abilities, and interests. Help the children to concentrate on what they *can* do and on the fun involved with exploring different hobbies or interests. Encourage the children to do their best in school and in other activities. All the while, be aware of the fine line between doing one's best and becoming so obsessed with doing well that no sense of enjoyment remains.

Most of us know adults who were made to do something they didn't want to do as kids, such as taking piano lessons. Instead of having fun with music, they ended up having a negative experience. Contrast this to a father Nancy once knew who took beginning piano lessons with his daughter so that they could have fun playing simple duets together. As an adult, the daughter still likes to play the piano for her own enjoyment.

 WHEN KEITH WAS ELEVEN, *his parents divorced and it hit the boy hard. His dad Jimmy left the house. Although Jimmy stayed in the same town, he traveled a lot in his work and Keith didn't see him much at first. At that time, Keith loved airplanes. He used to build model airplanes and read books about airplanes. The good thing was that Jimmy changed jobs when Keith was thirteen so that he could spend more time with his son. Jimmy would encourage Keith to pursue his interest by buying him model airplane kits for his birthday and Christmas. Keith's dad also started taking him to air shows where they watched pilots pull off stunts. The father and son even got to meet a couple of the pilots. This encouragement helped Keith make up his mind. Later he joined the Air Force after college*

and eventually achieved his dream—to fly planes. Keith thinks his dad was instrumental in steering him that direction. He's grateful to him for that.

TIP 27 | Practice Humility

Willingness to admit mistakes to your kids or your ex sets a good example. A person who is unpretentious evokes respect from others.

Humility is one of the most misunderstood qualities that people can possess, yet it's one of the most admired. This quality is misunderstood because many people equate humility with humiliation, which it is not. Actually, humility is not about degrading oneself, but instead about recognizing one's humanity.

As humans, we all have flaws and character defects. We also have strengths and virtues. Healthy humility is balanced. You can achieve it by making an honest self-appraisal of your true nature, looking at the good as well as the not-so-good qualities in yourself. Then you can just be real. You can admit to your flaws without trying to hide them. As long as people see that you're working on improving yourself, they will usually admire you for admitting your weaknesses.

Owning your mistakes takes courage because you're admitting to being fallible and exposing the parts of yourself that are not "perfect." By doing this, you're setting a valuable example for your kids in being real and authentic. By being willing to be humble, you will gain a new respect from your child.

THE DAY THAT ART AND HIS WIFE *Jessica got divorced, they drove together in her car to the courthouse where the judge and lawyers were waiting. Even though Art was convinced that divorce was the only solution in their marriage, he was still overcome with emotion. At a certain point, Art reached over, put his hand on Jessica's, and said, "I'm really sorry for my part in the way things have turned out between us." It was a simple gesture, and yet, she visibly softened. "You were really not such a bad husband," she said. Both of them were close to tears. During their marriage, it had been much easier for Art to see her imperfections than it was for him to see his own, so this was a huge step. Did this incident change anything? In a word, yes. The gesture was one thing that softened the hard division that had existed between Art and Jessica. Afterwards, Art found himself being less defensive of his faults when his daughter asked questions about the divorce.*

It's not enough just to love your kids. You have to tell and show them, over and over.

CHAPTER 5

Communicate Often: Vary the Method

If you want to stay bonded with your kids, you need to consider both the quality, as well as the quantity, of your communications with them. For example, you want quality interactions with your children, but if you're only talking to them every couple of 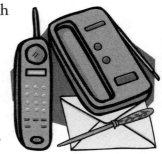 weeks, you really don't have the volume of connections you need to maintain a good relationship. So the number of times you talk to your children during a month is important. In addition, in order to avoid monotony in your messages, you'll want to vary the method of your communications.

Remember the saying that "Variety is the spice of life"? Variety in the ways you communicate with your kids is one of the means you can use to keep the excitement and fun in your relationship with them. Perhaps a child is looking forward to hearing from you, asking himself, "What will Dad do, say, or send me this week?" This is the type of response that you want.

Lee says, "We men sometimes overlook the nonverbal aspects of communication when interacting with our kids." One thing you can do is try methods of communication that appeal to a child's various ways of sensing the world, such as sight, sound, taste, smell, and touch. The following examples will show you how.

TIP 28 | Make Telephone Calls

This basic tool is essential for staying connected with your kids between visitations.

The effectiveness of staying close to your children by using the telephone will depend on the level of rapport you have already established. Also, this way of communicating will be less useful if there is difficulty in getting through when you call each other.

Perhaps you live in a different town that is a long-distance call away from your kids. If so, your ex-wife may be concerned about the cost of long-distance bills if your children want to call you frequently. With the price of long-distance calls coming down steadily in recent years, it's no longer a cost barrier to get your own toll-free number. By making it easy for your kids to contact you in this way, you'll hear from them more often. In fact, the wave of the future will be long-distance calls using the Internet for only a modest fixed amount per month. What you can get now for a reasonable cost is a variety of toll-free package deals from all of the major telephone companies.

6 Telephone Calling Tips

1. **Be aware of phone courtesy guidelines.** Try to be respectful of certain times, such as during dinnertime, when your children or your ex-spouse may not want to receive telephone calls. Do not call your kids after their bedtime or before they normally get up.

2. **Keep telephone conversations during the school week low-key.** In general, avoid any topics that might cause your kids to have trouble settling down after the phone call. Nancy has known numerous mothers who dread phone calls from their ex-spouses because the disruptive nature of the conversations upsets the kids for the rest of the evening.

3. **Be supportive of your ex-wife during your phone conversations with the children.** Unfortunately, some fathers use the opportunity provided by the phone call to grill their kids about minute matters and to be critical about how their ex-wives are handling things. This is damaging to your kids as well as to your efforts to create a team approach with your ex.

4. **If you call and the children don't want to talk, take the long-term view.** Everyone is moody at times, and kids are no exception. Teenagers, in particular, have raging hormones, which can cause wild swings in their willingness to talk. Rest assured that if your overall relationship with a child is solid, he'll want to chat with you later even if he doesn't talk with you right away.

5. **If the calls are long distance, check with at least three phone companies to find a good deal for a toll-free number so your kids can call you.** Once you have your toll-free number, it can be routed to your home telephone. The cost for the service at the time of this writing is only

about $5 a month plus a per-minute charge of just six to seven cents.

6. **Write your toll-free number on stickers and ask your kids to put them in an appropriate location.** That way, the number will always be handy if they want to make spontaneous calls to you.

TIP 29

Send Letters, Emails, or Faxes

Use these methods to share appropriate details of your life so your kids can relate to you.

Develop the habit of sending your children letters, emails, or faxes on a regular basis. Sending traditional letters by post takes more effort, but kids love to get mail. Most children don't receive a lot of mail addressed personally to them, so they will feel special and important when your letter arrives.

If you and your kids both have access to the Internet, communicating by email will be faster and easier. You can usually communicate more frequently by email, which allows you to share more details of your life. You might write about something that you would have forgotten by the time you got to talk over the phone or to visit in person. If a child is willing to answer back when you email her, you will have a greater chance of sharing more of the daily happenings in her life, too.

Two advantages of sending faxes are that they're immediate and no Internet connection is necessary. Of course, both parties need to have fax machines. One fun aspect is that pictures can be faxed, so you and your children could exchange drawings or other art work. Make sure the kids have your fax number if it's different from your telephone number. Young children will need help in operating the fax machine.

4 Tips for Letter Writing

1. **If you send conventional snail-mail letters, include a self-addressed stamped envelope** to make it easy for a child to respond.

2. **Consider sending a small surprise in the letter.** Examples are stickers or Pokemon cards.

3. **Make your child want to read your letters.** Let your true feelings show. Lee says, "It's been said that we men are like turtles—hard on the outside but soft on the inside." Be sure to express your feelings in some way with every message you send. A simple statement like "I'm proud of you" goes a long way with a kid.

   Encourage your children to do their best by offering encouragement and support.

4. **Send a child some appealing stationery that would be fun for someone his age to use.** You might also mail along some brightly colored or unusual pens. A child who is normally resistant might be coaxed into letter writing by a black notepad and a collection of gel pens that write in different colors on dark paper. Older kids may be intrigued by wax seals and calligraphy pens.

TIP 30 | Mail Greeting Cards

Conventional or email greeting cards using graphic design, humor, or sound effects can delight your children.

Send a child a cute, funny, or encouraging greeting card in the regular mail or by email when she is not expecting one. You can use cards to remember special occasions, such as birthdays, Valentine's Day, Halloween, Thanksgiving, Easter, Christmas or Hanukah, or New Year's.

Cards can deliver words of encouragement before a big test, spelling bee competition, science project deadline, music or dance recital, cheerleading auditions, or sports-team tryouts. A timely card can communicate the messages "I love you," "I'm thinking about you," "I care about you," "I'm proud of you," and "I believe in you."

Some email card sites will let you select accompanying music and add a personal note to the card. Many of the cards have characters or pictures with movement and special effects guaranteed to make your kids smile.

4 Tips on Sending Greeting Cards

1. Use *Chase's Calendar of Events* to find days of the year that are designated for specific themes (for example, Absolutely Incredible Kid Day on March 21). Then send cards that relate to the various themes. Check with your local library to find a copy of the book.

2. Include a personal message to your child about something in her life.

3. Send email greeting cards from different Internet sites. Email greeting card companies include BlueMountain.com, OhMyGoodness.com, Yahoo.com (click on "Greeting"), and xenus.com/postcard/age.htm.

4. If you want to be original, you can print your own cards using a computer. Several software packages are available that allow you to make customized cards that can be printed on card stock. These include Publishing Platinum 2002, The Print Shop Deluxe 12.0, American Greetings Creatacard Platinum 6.0, Hallmark Card Studio Deluxe 3.0, and Microsoft Picture It!

TIP 31 | Deliver Favorite Foods

Gifts of home-baked cookies or other delicacies are a fun way to bond with your kids.

If you're comfortable in the kitchen, try baking cookies for your children, even if you have never done this. Find out what types of cookies are their favorites. You might learn to bake the same type of cookies that your mother or grandmother used to make for you if they appeal to your kids.

Kitchen shops sell cookie molds if you want to make the kind of cookies that you decorate after they're baked. Otherwise, if you don't have a family recipe, a good chocolate chip or peanut butter cookie recipe may do the trick. Then ship the cookies to your children overnight if you live in a different town, or if you live in the same area, arrange with your ex to drop off this treat.

Home-baked items always carry the message, "I love you." The tradition you're starting now of occasionally sending home-baked goodies can continue as your kids mature. College students always love to get "care packages" from home, especially at exam time. So do grown children who join the military or move to another town to begin their working careers.

AFTER SALLY GRADUATED FROM HIGH SCHOOL, *she accepted a promising job offer in another state. Everything was tremendously exciting at first—finding an apartment, learning her way around, starting to work, and making new friends. But Sally also felt homesick more than she had expected, in spite of her divorced father's frequent phone calls and emails. One day, after a tiring day at work, Sally came home to find a package from her dad. Inside were two dozen of his special home-baked chocolate chip cookies. Her mouth watered just smelling them. Sally felt an immediate sense of being loved and valued by her father as she remembered the many times he had baked cookies during her childhood. Years later, Sally still remembers how much this gesture of love and support meant to her.*

TIP 32

Entertain with Jokes and Riddles

Laughter is the best medicine for stimulating a good mood.

Share appropriate jokes with your kids as you encounter ones that you think they would like. Many public libraries have joke books for children. You can find a useful book by asking the librarian in the children's reading section. Jokes can be sent to your kids through the postal mail or emailed. One advantage of email is that you can send a question, such as "Why did the chicken cross the road?" and a child can email back his answer before you provide the real response. You can also send "knock-knock" or other types of jokes that your children will enjoy repeating to their friends. Once you send a few of these, you will know from a child's feedback to you if he likes what you send him.

Riddles are also fun to share. A good source of riddles might be found in a book at the library, too. Email or the telephone are equally effective in sending riddles. Email has the advantage of allowing a child to think of the answer in her own time, whereas telephone riddles require an on-the-spot response. If you stimulate a child's curiosity, you'll have an excuse to call her to ask if she has the riddle's answer. Riddles force kids to think. You might offer a small prize if a child can solve the riddle you gave her.

Try alternating your approach in stimulating your kids to laugh and think. You can send a joke one week, followed by a riddle the next. If a child solves three riddles in a row, you could promise him an ice cream cone on his next visitation with you. A further challenge could be that you require him to send you a joke or a riddle. A variation would be that you alternately ask each other a riddle. Start with easy riddles and progress to more difficult ones.

3 Tips for Jokes and Riddles

1. **Find age-appropriate jokes and riddles** by looking in children's books and magazines.

2. **Remember that children's humor is different from adult humor.** Think back to what you found funny when you were a kid. In lower elementary school, Nancy remembers laughing with classmates over "knock-knock" jokes repeatedly until a teacher had to ban jokes from the classroom because of the constant disruption. These jokes don't seem funny to her now, but then they elicited much laughter.

3. **During visitations, ask your kids to share some of the jokes they have heard recently.** This will help you to keep up with your children's changing sense of humor.

TIP 33 | Give Well-Timed Photographs

Pictures of your kids taken at significant events or moments will mean a lot to them.

Always have a camera ready when you're with your children on an outing. In addition, take advantage of offers from others to take pictures of you and the kids.

If you can capture special moments either on film or digitally, you will profit doubly. First, you will have your own record of that time for you to remember and cherish with your children. Second, after you send your kids copies of the pictures, you have an excuse to call and ask, "Did you get the pictures?" and to comment on any shots that made you laugh.

 JIM HAD BEEN HAVING TROUBLE *getting his four-teen-year-old son Randy to open up and talk when Jim called him each week. Randy, it seemed, was just being a teenager, or so Jim thought. But then they went white-water rafting in North Carolina, and Jim had some photos taken of them as they crashed down a particularly wild section of the river. Both Jim and Randy were screaming with excitement at the time. The following week, Jim sent Randy a large, framed photo of the two of them in the raft with their mouths wide open. When Jim called his son to be sure the picture had arrived safely, Randy talked more than usual. In the months that followed, Randy was much more talkative about his life when Jim called.*

3 Options for Sending Photographs

1. **You can always send conventional photo prints by snail mail.** Even a disposable camera can give you acceptable prints at a reasonable price.

2. **You can email pictures taken with a digital camera.** To do this, first download the images from your camera to a file on your computer's hard disk, and then attach them to an email that you send to your kids.

3. **There's also a hybrid solution that uses pictures taken with a conventional camera.** You take your film to a lab that can develop it and then transfer the images to a CD Rom disk. Finally, transfer the pictures to MPEG files on your computer and attach them to emails.

   With Options #2 and #3, offer technical help to your ex and the children if they need it.

TIP 34

Collect News Items

Help educate your children with clippings from magazines and newspapers.

Note your kids' interests and then look for articles that relate to those topics. Childhood is the time when we learn the core habits that stay with us for the rest of our lives. If you set the example of staying informed about world and national events, your kids are more likely to do the same.

What interests do your children currently have? If you're not sure, ask the questions "What do you like to do?" "If you could travel anywhere in the world, where would it be?" "If you could be any animal, which one would you choose?" and "How would you spend your time if television and computer/video games were off limits?" A few of these questions should start to give you an idea of what types of clippings would be of most interest to your kids.

Then cut out a relevant newspaper or magazine story, xerox a copy for yourself, and mail the original to the child. For example, a kid who is interested in the Loch Ness Monster would enjoy a handwritten note with a newspaper article detailing recent attempts to find the elusive creature. Also, if you see a general news story that you think your child would find funny or amusing, send it. Develop the habit of being on the lookout for items that might appeal to your kids.

JERRY KNEW HIS TEN-YEAR-OLD SON KEVIN *had an interest in dinosaurs that had started when they went to see the movie "Jurassic Park" together. So in order to encourage Kevin's interest in science and the world, Jerry cut out newspaper articles on recent archeological finds in different countries. This way, Kevin got to learn not only about the large reptiles, but also about geography and the history of the earth. And it provided a topic for the two to talk about whenever Jerry called.*

TIP 35 | Mail Postcards

Picture postcards from places you visit show kids that you are thinking of them while you're away.

Send postcards to your children when you have to be away on business trips or travel for other reasons. Then they can see images of the places you have visited. This will be a way for them to learn about places outside of their hometown. They may also get a better idea of what your life is like and perhaps more of what your job entails. It could encourage them to travel.

Sometimes all your kids want from you is a reminder that they are important to you. You don't need to spend a lot of money to demonstrate your caring, however. A simple note on the back of a postcard will do, perhaps commenting on something they did recently. Always try to be positive and encouraging. A short message can be powerful. An example is the message "Thinking of you. I'm proud of you for that report card improvement. Love, Dad." Even if a child is struggling with schoolwork, any improvement is a step in the right direction. If you recognize her efforts, she will be motivated to continue. A simple postcard can help to accomplish this.

WHEN HARRY WENT ON A BUSINESS TRIP *to St. Louis, he sent Melinda, his twelve-year-old daughter, a postcard featuring a picture of that city's Gateway Arch. It was a quick and easy way for him to stay connected with Melinda in addition to a telephone call he had made after being away for several days. Harry had found the card for sale at the St. Louis airport while he was waiting for the flight home. He wrote a quick note on it and dropped the card in a postbox at the airport. Melinda appreciated the card most of all because it showed that her dad was thinking of her even when he was busy and away from home.*

TIP 36 | Visit Your Kids

A visit with your children in their hometown can mean a lot.

Although the court may have mandated formal times of visitation, it might be possible for you to see your kids at other times. If you live in the same town as your children, you have an advantage over a father who must travel some distance for a visit. You have more opportunities to see your kids in their natural setting and to know more about their daily lives. You may be able to see a child's performance in a school play, attend a child's soccer game, or take a short walk with your kids in a nearby park.

If you live elsewhere and normally have the visits at your house, consider traveling to your kids' hometown for one of your visitations. If you do not have family or friends who you can all stay with, rent a motel room. Select a motel with a swimming pool or other amenities, if possible. This will be a novelty for your kids and provide some entertainment. During your visit, ask your kids to show you the places where they routinely go, such as school, church, or music lessons. Also, plan an activity that includes some of your children's friends so that you can meet them. For example, you could arrange a picnic in the park, a pizza party, or a skating outing. If a child plays sports and there is a game during your visit, you'll be able to see him play and to meet his coaches. Have him introduce you to his teammates and meet their parents.

If you visit on a weekend during the school year, plan to arrive early on Friday or stay over until Monday evening. That way, you can meet your children's teachers. Use your visitation time to expand your knowledge of the network of people who support and instruct your kids.

ROBERT LIVED FOR A FEW YEARS IN FRANCE *because of his job, and while there he met a local woman. They fell in love, married, and had a daughter. Unfortunately, the marriage did not work out and Robert had to return to New York, leaving his daughter Joy behind with his ex-wife. However, he was determined to maintain a strong connection with Joy. His ex-wife brought Joy to the U.S. once a year, and Robert got to see her then, but that was not enough. Even though it was a 6,000 mile trip, he started visiting his daughter a couple of times a year in the city near Paris where she lived. The benefit was that Robert got to see Joy's school, meet her friends, and visit the places where she liked to go. It made all the difference in keeping their bond going. Now Joy is in her teens and can fly over to the States by herself to visit her dad. But without that special effort he made soon after the divorce, Robert doubts that they would be as close today.*

TIP 37 — Watch a TV Show Together Long Distance

Speaking on the phone while viewing a television program can be fun.

Watch a TV show with your kids while talking on the phone and commenting on the program. You can do this even if you are calling long distance. Just make sure you have a good calling plan with low-cost minutes. The children can take turns being on the phone with you.

In planning this, clear the day and the time with your ex-wife first. When you call that day, make sure that other members of her household are not expecting urgent calls. If it's more appropriate, you can talk for a fifteen-minute stretch, calling again later in the program or afterwards to discuss it further.

Ball games are a good example of TV programming you might share with the kids. To add to the excitement, you all could make predictions of what the score will be at the end of the game. The person with the closest guess might get a small prize. Make the prediction light and fun, without putting pressure on your kids, or otherwise they won't want to do this. Remember that the idea is not to compete, but to bond.

HENRY AND HIS FOURTEEN-YEAR-OLD SON Jeff both liked to watch football. One Saturday, Henry made arrangements with Jeff's mother to call Jeff during a game that he and his son were both interested in. To avoid tying up the phone line, Henry said he would call in both the second and fourth quarters of the game. That way, Henry and Jeff were able to recap and share with each other the most exciting parts of the game. It was enjoyable for both of them and brought the father and son closer together, which resulted in a more satisfying relationship later on.

TIP 38 | Review a Book Together

Conventional and audio books create an opportunity to learn and share.

This is likely to be an activity that's best to do with just one child. Find a book that interests both of you. It can be either fiction or nonfiction. You don't even have to buy the book, as you can each check out a copy from the local libraries. Set a deadline to finish reading the book. You might even offer the child a small incentive to encourage her to read it. Periodically ask her how she's enjoying the book. She may simply say, "Fine." Try to draw her out by asking questions like "What part of the book are you enjoying the most?" "Who is your favorite character in the book?" "Why do you think she did that?"

One of the greatest gifts you can give your kids is the habit of reading because it will open up vistas of opportunity to see the world through the eyes of the authors. By reading the same book simultaneously, you have the opportunity to bond with a child. And reading will help the child academically by expanding her vocabulary and her knowledge of the world.

If you're traveling a distance with the kids in the car, you can all enjoy an audio book together. You'll also find audio books at the library. The book you listen to will give you material for later discussions.

DAN'S DAUGHTER KELLY LOVES ANIMALS. *So Dan found a children's book with short stories about animals of different kinds. He bought two copies and sent Kelly one of them. They set a goal of reading so many stories between every phone call he made to her. Then they would discuss the stories. Because the stories were emotional, it helped Dan and his daughter with their own feelings about each other when they discussed the book. And because each story was short and stood alone, there was never any problem in reading at least one between phone calls. This exercise really helped Dan and Kelly stay close. And Dan was glad that this activity was encouraging Kelly to read.*

TIP 39	**Share Artwork**

Your kids will appreciate artwork you send that brightens their day.

You might try your hand at drawing some pictures yourself. It doesn't really matter if you are artistic or not. If you're not, it shows your kids that you're human, and it gives you the opportunity to laugh at yourself. It also shows the children that you are trying different ways to connect with them. You might even try drawing a picture related to something you had laughed at together.

When you do something that you're not naturally good at, such as drawing or painting, without getting uptight or embarrassed, you send an important message to your kids. That is, it's all right to attempt to do challenging things that take you out of your comfort zone. You are teaching them that it's okay to do something just for fun without worrying about being perfect or being judged.

When you've finished with your attempt, send it to your kids. Then call and find out if it was received. Ask your children how they might have done it differently. Ask if they could do it better. Again, remember that your goal is not to compete with your kids for artistic excellence. Rather, you're trying to bond, have fun, and perhaps even laugh at yourself. Humility in admitting your human limitations can be endearing.

JOHN WAS NOT ARTISTIC AT ALL. *In fact, when he tried to draw a picture of Mandy's dog running in the snow, the drawing came out looking like a three-year-old's artwork. He sent it to Mandy anyway, who was eight years old and was more practiced in drawing. Mandy laughed when she saw her dad's feeble attempt. When John called her soon afterwards, he was able to poke fun at himself about his inept skill. What surprised Mandy was her dad's willingness to show her what he had done even though the drawing wasn't well done. This gave Mandy permission to draw a picture for her dad without being embarrassed because it wasn't perfect.*

 TIP 40

Find a Comic Strip

A favorite comic strip will provide diversion and can be a pleasant surprise.

Children like to be visually stimulated. Since kids tend to like the characters from comic strips, perhaps your children read the funnies from the daily newspaper. Ask them what their favorite cartoon or comic book figures are. Then be on the lookout for a comic strip with one or more of these favorite characters in it that they haven't seen.

If a child likes one strip in particular, you might pick up an available comic book of the strip in a specialty comic book store. Or you might try going online and inputting "comics" or "comic books" in your search engine to find alternate sources that would sell you a book by mail order. You can have it shipped directly to a child via snail mail.

If you want to simply send your children a strip that you've cut out of the newspaper, there are several ways to send it, as the following box demonstrates. In each case, xerox the image first, whether to have a copy for yourself, to have a backup, or to make faxing easier.

4 Ways to Send Images

1. **Traditional Fax**—Using a traditional fax machine is a quick and easy way of sending images as well as text. The downside of this approach is that both parties need to have a fax machine.

2. **Internet**—Faxes can also be sent via the Internet by visiting www.efax.com and following the directions. There's a subscription fee of $9.95 per month, but the company allows you two free faxes for trying the service. This approach allows regular fax machines to send faxes to computers and vice versa. Since computers with access to the Internet are somewhat more common in the home than a fax machine, only one party needs a standard fax machine with this method. This way, however, is slightly more complicated than using two fax machines.

3. **Email attachments**—This approach involves scanning the artwork and then saving the scan as a .gif image in a file on your computer. Finally, you attach the file to an email that you send to your kids. This approach requires two computers connected to the Internet.

4. **Snail mail**—This is the old way of sending images and text. It works, but is slow. The good thing is that it requires no equipment.

TIP 41 | Give Keepsakes to Remember

Specific reminders of special moments or outings can strengthen your bond with your kids.

Send your children something that will remind them of a special time or moment when you felt close to each other. Perhaps a child particularly enjoyed eating barbecue on her last visit to see you. Send her the menu from the restaurant that you took the kids to in order to trigger pleasant memories of your last outing. Or maybe a child loves the local or regional baseball team where you live. Send him the program for a ball game you went to together. If you spent a wonderful week with the children camping out in the Smoky Mountains last August, send them some of the brochures you collected during your time together that will remind the kids of the trip highlights.

Any time you have a moment with your children that's worth remembering, look for keepsakes from the experience that you can send to them later. This simple act will bring back the memories of that time and make them think of the pleasure of being with you when the souvenirs arrive.

 During a spring break vacation *to the Gulf coast, Dennis took his twins to an aquarium to see some large fish and sea mammals. His kids were particularly intrigued by a tank of small sharks that were visible from above, and the twins loved the show where a woman riding on the nose of a killer whale splashed them with water. Dennis kept the program of all the events, along with a few postcards showing some of the seals and dolphins doing acrobatic tricks with the trainers.*

He surprised the twins several weeks after the vacation ended with a small scrapbook filled with reminders of the trip. It contained the program and postcards, a sand dollar taped in place, and a photograph that had been taken of the three of them, grinning and holding up some fish they had caught. It was a powerful reminder of the good experience they had shared.

TIP 42 | Use Instant Messaging

This feature on the Internet allows you immediate communication with your kids.

If you subscribe to an Internet service that offers instant messaging, you can interact in real time with your kids. Instead of having to open an email program when you are surfing, a message window pops up on your screen. This is a more spontaneous means of communicating with a child than email is. It can be fun to play word games, solve riddles, or tell jokes to each other using instant messaging. You can also use it to communicate in real time when watching the same television program.

If you find an interesting web site that would be of interest to a child, you can send him an instant message with the web address. If he doesn't already know how, teach him how to cut and paste a web address from an email to the window of his search engine to avoid typing in a long URL.

RON FOUND A WAY TO STAY CONNECTED *with Mark, his fourteen-year-old son, using instant messaging. Ron and Mark both loved to watch Monday Night Football, and they each had access to a computer conveniently located in front of a television set in their respective homes. Ron had been noticing that the announcers of the game had started polling viewers to vote online in real time on controversial referee calls. This gave Ron an idea. Since both he and Mark usually voiced strong opinions about such calls, instant messaging could provide them with a means of comparing opinions about particular calls as the officials were deciding on the outcome. To add fun to the contest, they eventually started to keep track of which one of them was correct more often in predicting the outcomes on such calls. Both Ron and Mark started looking forward to the instant messages they would send each other during games. It was yet another way for Ron to stay bonded with his son.*

A Tip for Using Instant Messaging

There are a number of Internet Service Providers (ISP) and other dot.com companies that offer instant messaging when you subscribe to their services. These include Yahoo, MSN, AOL, and Earthlink. You and your children will have to use the same service to guarantee compatible versions of instant messaging that will allow you to communicate this way.

Set Up a Family Email List

You can keep your kids informed with the same information about yourself that you broadcast to other family members

Perhaps you use Microsoft Outlook Express or a similar program to manage your lists of people you normally email. If there's information that you typically would like members of your family to know, such as getting a new dog or painting your house a different color, you can easily broadcast the news via your computer. One of the wonders of computer technology is that you can write one message, and with a few clicks of your mouse, email it to as many people as are on your list.

You might consider starting a family email newsletter. To do so, you would first create a family email list on Outlook Express that includes the email addresses of the relatives you want to stay in touch with. The list might consist of the addresses of your parents, your siblings, and your nieces and nephews. Add your kids' email addresses to this list so that they also get the latest news you're sending to everyone else. This will make your children feel a stronger part of the family. In one easy step, you can keep your kids informed about events that are happening in your life. In today's world, when people are so strapped for time, this is a major advantage. Many times, if a father cannot find the time to communicate adequately with his children between visits, eventually he'll let that part of his relationship with them slide.

WHEN BERT HAD BEEN MARRIED, *it was his wife who actually wrote to his extended family to tell them of the events that were happening. In the four years since his divorce, Bert had largely fallen out of touch with his relatives. Then, when Bert got a new computer, he learned of the email broadcasting feature in a computer class at the local community college. Now, in just a few minutes every week, Bert writes a short message and broadcasts it to everyone in his family who is on his list. When he added his kids' addresses to the list, Bert found that they appreciated being informed about what was happening with him.*

What's some relevant news that your family would like to know about you? Perhaps you're looking for a new house and will be changing neighborhoods. Maybe you have found a better job and are shifting your work schedule, which could affect your visitation schedule with your kids. Your children need to know what is happening in your life. By all means, keep your kids in the information loop. Use technology to your advantage to save time and effort in staying connected with them.

> It's sharing the small details in your life that allows your kids to really know and stay connected to you.

Become the Family Webmaster

You can share family photographs with your kids instantaneously by posting them on your own web site.

The Internet has spawned a number of alternative ways of communicating and sharing photographs and other information electronically, without the hassle of sending letters and pictures by snail mail. While you may already know about using email attachments to send photographs, there's also another way that you can show photos and other information to your kids by using Internet technology.

Particularly if there are a relatively large number of people who you would like to inform about family affairs, you might consider building your own web site. This is a good way to communicate when you have extended family members (for example, your parents, brother, sister, nephews, nieces, cousins, etc.) who may be interested in seeing the photos that you post. A benefit is that you encourage members of your extended family to stay informed about your kids, and vice versa, when anyone in the family goes to your web site. This is good for your children. When people bond with relatives at a young age, they're more likely to keep those family connections later. Plus, it further cements your children's connection to you.

As you tell various family members about the web site, encourage them to email you about important events in their lives, which you can upload to the site. Then, as different family members respond to your request for information, continue to expand your site. You might also post your kids' photographs from your last vacation together. Then tell your children to look at the site whenever they want. Using the family web site, your kids will get to know the extended family better, and they, in turn, will learn more about your kids.

Web Site Building Tips

There are many dot.com companies that offer hosting services for a web site. Two that still offer free web hosting are MyFamily.com and Geocities.com. You get from 5 to 15 megabytes of memory to play with in showing your family pictures. Since photographs, movies, and audio files tend to take up a lot of storage, you can pay for more disk space on the hosting service if you decide to use any of these features on your site. Web sites are a semipermanent way of displaying any family information you have. Your site becomes a virtual photographic gallery and family archive, open to whomever you tell about it.

TIP 45 | Provide Your Children with a Pager and a Cell Phone

By giving your kids the tools that will allow you to stay in touch, you remove all excuses for not remaining in close communication.

With the prices of today's tools for staying in touch going down, it's becoming increasingly affordable to consider getting a beeper and/or a cell phone for your children. Offer to pay for the airtime when the phone is used for talking with you. You can allot a budget of so many minutes per month by periodically buying a calling card with a fixed number of minutes of prepaid airtime.

Prepaid calling cards are a popular way for parents to budget their children's usage of cell phones. Some cellular plans even offer free call reception. That way, you can call your kids as much as you like without having to pay for their phone usage. The ease and convenience of calling can make a major difference in how often you get to talk with your children. If your kids are old enough to use the phone responsibly, this is an option you should consider.

CHRIS HAD PROBLEMS IN CALLING *his ex-wife's number to talk with the kids. It was sometimes inconvenient for Chris to call in the evenings due to his work schedule. And even when he did call, the children were often out of the house, eating dinner, or doing homework. Furthermore, his ex frequently let the answering machine respond instead of picking up the phone or checking caller ID due to the number of telemarketers who called every evening. Chris decided to purchase cell phones and beepers for both of his teenaged sons. Now he talks to each of them several times each week, and his sons call him more often. The benefits to all have been substantial.*

❖ ❖ ❖

CHAPTER 6

Support Learning: Make Acquiring Knowledge Fun

Kids are naturally curious and want to learn. That is, unless they have been discouraged by some experience at home or school. In today's world, success in life so often depends on what people know. So promoting the enjoyment of learning to your children is an important way you can help them.

Encourage your kids by making learning through both experience and reading fun, rewarding, and supported. You can make learning enjoyable for your children by encouraging such opportunities in their areas of interest. For example, if your son likes antique cars, find a book at the library on the subject. If your daughter enjoys working with modeling clay, enroll her in an art class.

Offer to help with school homework during visitations at your home. Encourage your kids to start on big school projects early and not to wait until the last minute. Help them to organize the various components of an assignment, such as doing a science fair project, and to develop a time line for finishing it.

Dads need to be actively involved. Your help and support can be invaluable as you look for opportunities to make the learning process enjoyable for your kids. Offer your help, support, and encouragement so that they can do their best. Be generous with praise regarding schoolwork or independent projects when your child has done something that deserves recognition.

TIP 46 — Make the Initial Contact with the School

Getting off on the right foot with teachers will save you and your children headaches.

At the first of each school year, initiate contact with your children's school. Call the principal and express your desire to be actively involved in your kids' education. Ask for a copy of the school calendar, your children's classes and teachers, and information about any planned special events. Find out the names of the school counselors and the best way to make contact. Ask about any extracurricular activities that your kids can choose to pursue, such as clubs, sports, the school newspaper, or the yearbook. Also request that the school send you copies of all of your children's report cards, progress reports, discipline write-ups, and standardized test scores during the school year.

The first time you call, you'll probably be asked to mail or fax a copy of the divorce custody agreement so that the school will have it for their records. This is just the standard procedure, so don't take offense at the request. Put your energy into developing a productive, efficient working relationship with the principal, school counselors, and other school personnel so that you can readily obtain the information you'll need about your kids' academic performance and behavior. Let those at the school know that you're a concerned parent who wants to support the school's efforts to provide a quality education for your children. Also state that when your schedule permits, you plan to visit the school and are looking forward to meeting the principal, counselors, and teachers.

After you make contact with the kids' school principal, call and introduce yourself to your kids' school counselors and teachers. *Express to the counselors and teachers your intent to be an involved parent, and tell them that you want to be supportive of your children's educational experience.*

4 Tips for Helping Your Kids Succeed Academically

1. Be consistent in your contact with your children's teachers.

2. Follow through on any assistance to your kids that you agree to give.

3. Let your children know, through your weekly phone conversations and emails, that you are keeping current about their grades.

4. Offer your own incentives for increased effort, good study habits, and acceptable grades. The incentive could be something that you and a child would do together on your next visit, such as going to the zoo, attending a favorite sporting event, or eating at your child's favorite restaurant.

Seek Feedback from Your Kids' Teachers

A requirement of really helping your children is to have accurate information.

Seek feedback from school teachers, coaches, and other instructors of any extracurricular classes (for example, art, language, band, etc.). Talk with them, but be careful not to be defensive if some of the information about your kids is negative. Try to adopt the attitude that negative feedback is an opportunity to look closely at your children's current behavior or abilities and to use this information to help them improve. Keep in mind that you're not helping a child by denying the areas he needs improvement in.

Ask your kids' teachers to send you a weekly email letting you know how the children are doing academically and behaviorally, and to also send a copy of the email to your ex-spouse. When you send emails to the teachers, also send copies to your ex so that she will know your concerns or reactions. Ask what long-term projects your kids will have to complete during the school year and decide if you can supervise some of them long-distance. Coordinate this with your ex-wife. In addition, ask the teachers for any recommendations they have about how you can encourage your kids to do their best in school.

Not all schools will be accustomed to accommodating noncustodial fathers in this way, but do not let that discourage you from requesting to be involved. Share with the representatives of the school that you're doing this so that you can be a more supportive, actively involved parent, and remind them that your actions will have positive benefits for your children. Be sure to share with the teachers any information about changes in your life that will affect the kids, such as your being remarried, the arrival of a new baby, or plans to move to another part of the country.

LIZ FELT LIKE SHE WAS ALWAYS THE "BAD GUY" *when it came to supervising her son's homework and academic progress. Each time report cards were sent, her ex-husband Ron would grill her on the phone about their son's grades and why these weren't better. After talking with a counselor, Liz decided it would be beneficial to talk with Ron about being directly involved in the communication loop with the school. She asked him to contact a teacher, and Ron agreed to do so. Luckily the teacher, Rose, was supportive of Liz's efforts, and Rose began to send emails to Ron each week, letting him know how his son was doing. Ron appreciated being more closely involved in his son's schoolwork. Liz felt relieved that the pressure was off her shoulders about being the person in the middle between her ex-husband and the teacher. As a result of their new approach, Ron and Liz have improved their ability to function as a parenting team, and their son's grades are steadily improving.*

Be Aware of Your Own Baggage

Helping your kids succeed in school sometimes may mean confronting the baggage from your own academic experience. This can include being bullied, making poor grades, disliking school, or being disciplined. Don't let your own negative memories keep you from being an involved parent now.

| TIP 48 | **Visit the School When Possible** |

If you're proactive in meeting your children's scholastic mentors, you increase the chances of their maximum cooperation in communicating with you about your kids.

Make a special effort to plan a trip to meet your children's teachers, school counselors, and principal, even if you live a considerable distance away. If you can, time your trip so that you can help with a class program, party, or other special function. If you cannot time your trip to do this, volunteer to help with the expenses of an activity during the school year, such as a class party, pizzas during a field trip, or the end-of-the-year celebration.

There's no substitute for firsthand involvement in your children's lives, even if you're living at a distance from them. In order to relate to what your kids are experiencing each day, you need to have personal contact with their teachers, school counselors, and the school administrators. Your working relationship with school personnel will be greatly strengthened if you make it a priority to meet them in person and express your appreciation for all they're doing to help your kids. You will usually learn more from a face-to-face conference than any other way.

AFTER HIS DIVORCE, WALTER AT FIRST WAS HESITANT *to contact the officials at his son's school. After all, he had never dealt with Jack's school matters. That had been something his former wife Sandra had always done. But*

Walter recognized that with Sandra having to take a full-time job now to make ends meet, she would have less time to make phone calls and visits to Jack's teachers. So Walter bit the bullet and called Jack's school. He asked to set up an appointment for his day off the following week to meet with Jack's teacher to discuss grades and study habits. Walter requested that the school counselor attend the meeting so that he could discuss some fights Jack had gotten into on the playground. Thereafter, for the remainder of the school year, Walter periodically kept in touch with the school staff. He also talked to Jack weekly about his schoolwork. Jack's grades improved as a result of Walter's attention, and the school counselor reported that Jack seemed to be getting along better with his schoolmates.

How Can a School Counselor Help?

Contacting a child's school counselor is an important step to take. School counselors can serve as valuable liaisons between parents and teachers or other school personnel. If you have a concern about a child's grades or behavior, the school counselor can obtain feedback from teachers, analyze standardized test scores, review grades and conduct, talk to the child, and then make recommendations. If a teacher conference is indicated, the school counselor can help you schedule the meeting. School counselors are used to handling situations involving divorced parents. They can be of great assistance to you in coordinating your efforts with those of your ex-wife. In additional to offering individual counseling, many school counselors also offer group counseling for students with similar needs on topics such as how to cope when parents divorce, how to make friends, and how to manage anger.

TIP 49

Go on an Educational Outing

By accompanying a child's class on a field trip, you show your resolve to be involved in the child's academic success.

If you can arrange to take time off from work, volunteer to be one of the parents who helps to chaperone a child's class on a field trip. You will get to know the teacher better and perhaps meet some of the child's classmates as well. Parents of other students in the child's class will probably also be chaperones, so you may have a chance to get to know them also.

Volunteering in this way makes a statement to your child that you care enough about her to make time for special events. It also makes a statement to your child's teachers that you are serious about being involved in her academic life. A benefit to you is that you'll get to learn more about how the child interacts with her friends and classmates at school, plus you will get to hear any feedback that is offered about her from the teacher or other parents. It always helps to have the opportunity to observe a child firsthand and to know as much about her world as possible.

 WHEN JUDY WAS A CHILD, *her class went to the Children's Theatre once to see a production of "Pinocchio." Judy's dad had volunteered to take a day off from work to come with the class and help the fourth-grade teacher, Mrs. Riley. This trip was a turning point for Judy and her dad.*

Judy's parents had divorced when she was two, and after that, her dad had moved to another town. She did not see her father very often because he traveled as a salesman and rarely visited Judy. When she was nine, he told her that he was moving

back to Judy's hometown for good. Her dad said that he'd been "sick" for a long time from drinking too much, but had gotten help and was doing better now. Judy remembers thinking that he'd changed somehow and was different from the way she remembered him. When she was little, he used to fight with her mom whenever he would come to pick Judy up. Now he seemed more quiet and calmer.

Judy felt the best thing about that morning of the field trip was how her dad held her hand in front of the whole class as they walked together and then entered the theatre. She noticed that her father smiled a lot and held his head up like he was proud of Judy. That was the last time anyone at school teased Judy about not having a dad. It was the first time Judy felt she really had one.

Help Develop Accountability

When you teach this life skill, your kids learn responsibility.

It can be challenging for a parent to find the right balance between encouraging the children to do their best and not accepting excuses for poor performance versus being too unrealistic, perfectionistic, or demanding. A parent who permits a child to always blame someone else or some other contributing cause is doing the child a disservice. So is the parent who is accepting of a child's academic laziness and half-hearted efforts. Kids need encouragement to do their best and to keep on trying even when they do not see instant results.

If allowed to do so, kids can easily develop the habits of rationalizing their behavior, denying responsibility, and blaming others. Children also easily develop the habit of procrastinating and not starting to study for tests soon enough. They might wait until the last minute and then discover that there's not enough time left to study thoroughly. Kids may also habitually put off preparing for book reports and doing big projects until the night before the assignments are due.

Needless to say, children who don't learn self-discipline and develop good study habits are at a disadvantage in school. Here's where you could help because praise from a father can be a powerful motivator for a child. You can be supportive by finding strengths in a child to praise, and by encouraging the child's efforts to do his best. You can also be of assistance by keeping current about what the child is doing in school, what tests and projects are coming up, and what grades he is making weekly.

Support the Use of Natural Consequences

Be supportive of your ex-wife's efforts to encourage your children to study and to take homework and grades seriously. Back her up when she has to discipline a child for not completing an assignment or turning homework in late. You may not agree with her choice of discipline, but if you have created a solid team approach, you can discuss this privately with her. The important thing is not to undermine her efforts. *Always support the idea of natural consequences that follow actions.* For instance, if your daughter lies about not having any homework to do and watches TV instead of studying, a natural consequence would be for her to be grounded from television watching for a period of time. Or if your son's teacher is complaining that he is falling asleep in the first period class each day, a natural consequence would be for the son to have to go to bed earlier. *The goal is for your kids to learn to take responsibility for their actions and to develop the self-discipline that it will take to accomplish life goals.*

TIP 51 | **Encourage Learning**

When you teach your kids to love to learn, you set them up for success in life.

Children need to be encouraged to learn as much as they can. There are plenty of negative distractions that can divert a child's attention away from reading and studying. You can help prevent that from happening. You may even be the primary person who fosters your children's love of learning.

STEVE'S PARENTS HAD DIVORCED *when he was very young, and when Steve was only ten, his dad passed away. The father had not had much of a formal education, but Steve remembers that his dad had read a lot. After this death, Steve's mother was overwhelmed with trying to work and raise five kids. Despite her efforts, the family had to go on welfare for a time. Steve got a job delivering newspapers to help out. He was the oldest child, and throughout those early years, it would have been easy for him to follow the example of some of the neighborhood kids. The family lived in a tough neighborhood, and there were drugs and gangs that some of his friends got involved in. Throughout that period, Steve kept remembering what his Dad had taught him—love reading, fill your head with knowledge, get an education. Steve let his father's voice talk him through high school while he bagged groceries nights and weekends. He let the voice comfort him while waiting tables though undergraduate years in college. Finally, the day that Steve graduated from medical school, he bowed his head and whispered back, "Thanks for your help, Dad. At last, we made it."*

All Learning Doesn't Come from Books

- **Life skills will help your kids succeed as much as book learning.** Take the time to teach your children social skills. Good manners will help them navigate in our society. These skills will even give your kids an edge on the job after they are grown.

- **Teach your children problem-solving skills** so that they know how to figure out the best solutions when they're not sure what to do. Share with them how you make decisions and handle crisis situations.

- **Encourage your kids to do crossword puzzles and word games.** These will help to increase their vocabulary skills and mental agility. Two good sources are *Children's Word Games and Crossword Puzzles, for Ages Seven to Nine* (Eugene T. Maleska) and *The Outrageous Crossword Puzzle and Word Game Book for Kids* (Helene Hovanec, Will Shortz).

TIP 52 | ## Support Goals and Dreaming

Show your kids that it's all right to set their sights high and to dream big.

Encourage your children in a few select areas, but don't expect them to do everything. Ask your kids what activities or hobbies they would like to do, and be supportive of these interests. Don't try to force them to do what you would do because this will not work. Different people have different strengths and interests, and theirs may not be the same as yours. Also, point out strengths and abilities that you notice they have.

Be realistic with your kids when you talk with them about their dreams and goals. Too often children hear the statement, "You can be anything you want to be," but they don't realize that wanting to be something is not enough. A child also has to be willing to work hard to achieve his goals. So it's more realistic to say, *"You can be anything you want to be if you're willing to work hard."*

For you to help your child develop a vision of what he can be and accomplish in his life, it helps to have a vision of your own possibilities. So stay responsible to yourself in your own life while also helping your child to see his potential.

4 Tips on Encouraging Goals

1. **Talk with your kids about their goals and dreams.** Make sure you're not imposing your own goals on your children. If you always wanted to be a doctor and are now urging a child to enter medical school, watch out! This may not be fair to the child, and it could damage your relationship with each other. Pay attention to what is right for each child.

2. **Always encourage the children to be curious about lifetime career possibilities.** Give them freedom to pursue productive hobbies and interests.

3. **When you call your kids between visitations, encourage brainstorming and dreaming.** Tell them that their imagination and willingness to work hard are the keys to success for the future.

4. **Teach your children not to be afraid of failure.** Treat failure as an opportunity to learn what does not work. Show the kids how to learn from feedback so that they can adjust their approach the next time.

Help with School Projects

The interest you take in your children's academic work emphasizes its importance.

Before the beginning of a new academic school year, talk to your kids' future teachers about the areas of study and large, long-term projects for the coming year. To find out who your children's new teachers will be, contact the school principal at the end of a school year before the summer break. If the teacher assignments have not been made yet, then talk to the principal or to the current teachers about what activities would help to prepare your children for the next grade. The goal is to find out ahead of time what your kids will study in school the coming year, especially in science and social studies. That way, you can try to connect the topics to the real world through the activities you do and trips you take together during visits.

You could talk to your ex-wife about your goal of volunteering to supervise one or more of the long-range projects or deeper learning in an area of study. For example, you might decide to supervise a child's science project while your ex-wife assumes responsibility for overseeing the social studies project. Then during your summer visitations, you might engage the child in science-related activities, like visiting the natural history museum, going on a field trip to study animals at the zoo, looking for butterflies in the countryside, or exploring an aquarium. You could also use the Internet to find out more information, and share it with the child.

Then when school starts again, help the child plan a timeline for working on and completing the academic project you're supervising. Check in with her regularly to be sure she is doing each task according to schedule. Monitor the child's progress and the quality of her work. This is an opportunity for you to teach the child how to break a large project down into small steps so that it's manageable. It is also an opportunity for you to demonstrate your ability to be consistent, dependable, and reliable in following through with what you said you would do in offering to supervise the project.

JIM TOOK HIS DAUGHTER JULIE ON A FIELD TRIP *to a primitive part of their state to look for fossils on several occasions. In the deep backwoods, they had the opportunity to observe nature and to be in the peace of the wilderness. Jim and Julie saw an armadillo crashing through the underbrush. They found deer and raccoon tracks by a streambed. The two cautiously watched a water moccasin slither out of the water and into the tall grass. Kneeling on a bed of water-polished pebbles, Jim and Julie spotted sharks' teeth that were at least 20 million years old. Julie was later able to take the teeth to school to show to her teachers and to her friends. Jim noticed that the field trips had helped arouse Julie's enthusiasm in the following year for doing school projects. Now she's already thinking ahead to next summer's visitation, and Jim and Julie are making plans to start a bug collection for the next year's science contest.*

5 Tips for Dealing with School Personnel

1. **Be tolerant of "phone tag" experiences** that you may have in trying to contact your children's principal or teachers. It will often take several attempts to reach the person due to factors related to the school environment.

2. **Be persistent in your efforts** to obtain the information you have requested or to talk to the person you're calling. If you don't hear back in a reasonable time period, follow up with another contact attempt.

3. **Be polite and courteous in your interactions** with school administrators, teachers, and other school personnel. Conditions are often hectic in school offices, and principals and secretaries handle many requests and deliver numerous messages every day. In this process, sometimes things get "lost in the shuffle." This can be frustrating, but being labeled as an angry, unreasonable parent will not help you to forge a productive working relationship with the school.

4. **Always try to resolve issues with the person you're dealing with before you consider going to a higher authority to complain.** If an issue is serious enough to go up the chain of command, be sure that you try each level in order. For example, let's say you have an issue concerning a teacher and you haven't been able to resolve it with him in spite of your attempts to do so. The next appropriate step is to talk to the principal. Going to the Superintendent's Office or Board of Education is a last step. Principals resent parents who go over their heads without giving them a chance to resolve things first.

5. **Consider how any actions that you take will impact your children and your relationship with your ex-spouse.** Kids are usually embarrassed if a parent unleashes anger at school personnel, and an ex-spouse who has tried to have a good relationship with the school will be upset if that relationship is jeopardized. Whether it's fair or not, what you do *does* affect the impression that principals and teachers have of your kids and it can make a difference in whether or not they feel comfortable in communicating with you.

❖ ❖ ❖

CHAPTER 7

Plan Vacations/Visits Together: Start the Process Early

There's a tendency for fathers to try to make up for lost time when they're with their kids. This can mean trying to cram as much experience as possible into each visit or vacation. To make up for not having more time with their kids, divorced dads may believe that they need to provide super-exciting trips and lavish gifts. But what is it that a child will remember the most twenty years from now? It will be that you taught her how to fish, helped him build a model airplane, or camped out with the children in the mountains one long, leisurely July 4th weekend. What counts more than extravagant gestures that cost money is the rapport that you build with your kids. This is what truly creates the bond that you and your children want.

So keep some perspective about what's really important about your visits together. "Disneyworld dads" go for lavish vacations and plans, spending a lot of money trying to create a great experience for their kids. This is not necessary. It's really the little things that count. Try "just hanging" with your kids. Do normal things around the house that your child can participate in. Turn off the television. Do yard work. If you're so inclined, fix something in the garage. Let a child watch. If appropriate, encourage him to help you. This may not sound like you're doing much, but the point is not to constantly entertain. What you want is to create experiences that allow the two of you to bond.

During vacations, you can maximize the value of your time with your kids by paying attention to what would be good for them as well as fun. Children enjoy doing new things, such as horseback riding, mountain biking, or going deep-sea fishing. Learning new skills and traveling to new places help children gain self-confidence. At the same time, they're gaining exposure to the world that will help them academically and personally.

You can also use visits and vacations to nurture your children's relationships with the people who are or who could be important in their lives now and in the future. These individuals might be extended family or simply friends who pay attention to your kids. When your children are with you, schedule quality time with family and friends. If you travel during a vacation together, visit with any family or friends who live along your travel route.

Select Activities to Do

TIP 54

Choosing the right things to do during your visits and vacations will make your time together a hit.

Visits and vacations are about enjoying free time and entertaining yourself and your kids. In addition, they can also be about providing your children with educational experiences suitable to their ages and maturity levels. You can check with a child's teachers to find out what kinds of activities or travel destinations would help him to be better prepared for what he's studying at school.

The activities that you plan do not have to be expensive, and many of the most memorable activities for children do not cost much. You could set up a tent in a nearby state park and invite a child's friend to join the two of you in camping out, building a fire, toasting marshmallows, and telling ghost stories. Or you could set up a bull's eye in the backyard and teach your kids how to use a bow and arrow. Other inexpensive activities to consider are hiking, fishing, and swimming. If there's a nearby lake, river, or reservoir, you could rent a paddle boat, rowboat, kayak, or canoe for a few hours. Bike shops often rent mountain bikes, which can provide hours of fun. You might decide to visit local museums or historical sites.

The starting place in planning activities for visitations or vacations is to know what your kids like to do or are interested in learning. Talk with them about the various choices and get their reactions and suggestions. Make planning your time together an interactive process before the visitation. There's always room for compromise if you don't agree immediately. If a child doesn't want to do something that you feel strongly is important for him, then build in a fun activity for him before or after it.

Ted was tired of feeling that he had to be a constant social director during visits with his kids. Feeling pressured to keep things moving, he was always very stressed by the end of a visit. Ted decided to talk with his children about their interests. He called and asked them to pick the five things they most wanted to do. Ted added that he would spread all the activities out over time. In subsequent visits, Ted planned fewer activities. He found that he enjoyed the time with his children more. He especially liked having time to relax and to do things at a more leisurely pace. Ted also enjoyed being able to do some home projects with his kids, such as building a bike ramp, planting flowers, and painting some outdoor furniture. He felt good about teaching them new skills.

TIP 55 | Send Information about Your Vacation Plans

Brochures and pamphlets on a vacation destination can stir anticipation and excitement.

You can prime your kids for a vacation by sending them information ahead of time. Spark their interest by sharing the history of the destination place, as well as the major sights to see and things to do. This can fire the children's imagination and add to their anticipation of the trip.

Try using the Internet to find out information. Does your destination have a web site? Contact the local tourist information center and request brochures and pamphlets. In addition, the National Park Service provides information on national park sites, lodgings, and activities offered in the various parks. Also, books available in the travel section of bookstores or at the library can provide useful information. You can send the background on the trip to your kids, or you may prefer to read key passages during phone conversations.

If you're excited about your plans, the children will be more likely to be excited too. The more your kids see you being open to learning new skills, doing new things, and traveling to new places, the more likely it is that they will develop the same attitude. The resulting openness to new experiences will help them be better prepared for life in a rapidly changing world.

AFTER ALLEN AND HIS SON KYLE DECIDED *to go camping during spring break, Allen called the National Park Service for some information about their destination, Sequoia Caverns. Allen knew that Kyle loved to learn about things related to Indians, since their family had ancestors who were Native Americans. A few days later, Kyle received a brochure by mail that the Park Service had sent upon his father's request. The brochure on Sequoia Caverns stated that it was a beautiful location near the place where the great Cherokee chief, Sequoia, had invented the written language of his people. Kyle also learned that Sam Houston, the first president of the Republic of Texas, had actually lived there for a time with his wife, a young Indian woman. This information whetted Kyle's appetite for the trip.*

TIP	**Use a Map**
56	*Sending appropriate maps will allow your kids to plot the milestones of your upcoming trip.*

Once you've decided on where you're taking the children for a vacation, send them a map with the route marked. You might buy a standard map from a book store, gas station, or convenience store. Another option is to use one of the new software products on CD Rom that allows you to print out maps of locations throughout the United States. With the CD Rom software, you have your choice of several levels of detail.

Ask your kids to look at the map and tell you what alternative routes you could take and what sights and towns you would encounter along the new route. Depending on their ages, you might ask them to also calculate the difference in distance, if any, between the two routes. And while you're traveling, let the children help you figure out directions by using the map.

If possible, buy the kids a large wall map of the U.S. that can be attached to a cork bulletin board. Encourage them to put "push pins" in the locations where they have traveled with you. If this is not possible, you and the children might use a bright marker to highlight the travel routes and places you have visited together.

BILL WANTED HIS TWO SONS TO UNDERSTAND *where they were going for a two-day camping trip. They had decided to hunt for Civil War relics during their vacation. For years, Bill had heard that a small river near his hometown had been the site of a Civil War skirmish. With the help of a history book from the library, Bill was able to zero in on a bend of the river where the conflict had been fought. Bill found a software program called DeLorme's Street Atlas USA. Using it, he was able to print out a color map that included the exact bend in the river described in the history book. Bill and his sons studied the map and found the skirmish site on it near the ruins of an old bridge. After getting the permission of the property's owner, Bill took the boys to the site, and they actually dug up a few miniballs from the conflict by using a metal detector. Later Bill's sons highlighted the area they had visited on a map and hung it on their bedroom wall. Bill's sons considered the experience a treasure hunt, and they wrote essays at school about the experience.*

TIP 57 | ## Take Your Children to a Family Reunion

By introducing your children to the extended family, you give them relationships that can last for the rest of their lives.

Make a special effort to stay connected with your own siblings and extended family members, and let your children get to know them too. If there are other kids in the family close in age to your children, try to arrange for them to spend time together at least once a year. This can be challenging when families live a great distance from each other. However your kids will benefit greatly by feeling closely connected to their cousins, aunts and uncles, and grandparents.

Attending reunions can help your children to have a greater knowledge of the extended family and its history. If your family does not have formal planned reunions, talk with your relatives about picking a date and place to meet during a time when your kids will be with you. Explain that you want your children to have a strong bond with others in the family, and that it's important enough to you that you are volunteering to help with the arrangements. As your children grow up, one of the treasures of their lives will be these special connections forged in childhood.

KATY'S EARLIEST MEMORIES OF VACATIONS *with her dad after the divorce included family reunions. At the reunions held at the grandparents' house, she got to know some of her cousins. Katy remembers how they used to push each other on a rope swing that hung from a huge oak in the grandparents' back yard. Years later, having lost touch with the majority of the cousins, Katy found herself in Tampa for business. On a whim, she looked up her cousin, Linda, who she had not seen in decades. Katy ended up staying with Linda at her house, and they had a blast catching up on family and sharing experiences of their lives. Looking back on this experience later, Katy felt so grateful that her dad had made a special effort to allow her to connect with the cousins at a young age. Finding Linda had been like locating a long-lost sister.*

Ordinary family get-togethers can make extraordinary memories for your child.

TIP 58 | **Make Signs and Give Places Names**

Using physical reminders of a child's place in your life will make her feel valued.

Name something at your house for a child when you are together, such as "Becky's lake," "Becky's pond," "Becky's tree," "Becky's garden," "Becky's swing," "Becky's room," or "Becky's playground." Have a cute sign made and display it prominently.

Doing this will make the child feel really special. It will also give her a sense of ownership for the place where you live. By naming a designated place at your home for the child, you anchor your home in her mind.

Take a picture of the sign in its special place so that she can look at the photo and show her friends after she returns to her mom's house.

Whenever Billy would visit his dad's house, the boy would always sleep in the spare bedroom. John was worried that his son Billy wouldn't feel that the bedroom was really his. And there had been times in the past when visiting relatives had to sleep in the spare bedroom when Billy wasn't there. John decided to name the room for his son, and he had a special sign made for the door. Since Billy liked dinosaurs, the sign read "Billy's Dinosaur Preserve." Billy was surprised and excited when he saw the sign. In addition, his dad also periodically added items to Billy's room related to dinosaurs. The room at his dad's house began to have a special significance to Billy, and he looked forward to reentering his "Dinosaur Preserve" on each visit.

❖ ❖ ❖

Everyday moments with your child can become your most cherished memories when captured in photos.

CHAPTER 8

Take Pictures: Use Your Camera Effectively

The old saying that a picture is worth a thousand words can apply to keeping in touch with your kids. A photograph can bring back memories more easily than mere words. For this reason, both you and your children will find special meaning in taking and keeping photos of events that all of you will want to remember and treasure. The photographs can be preserved not just on photographic paper, but also on a variety of things like mugs, posters, and T-shirts.

There are many ways you can use pictures to bond with your children. Pictures of things that have meaning to a child often communicate more than words can. Think of a time when you were alone with a child. Perhaps you were not doing anything special, but you were both enjoying being together. Maybe something happened that made you and the child laugh. It may have been totally unexpected, but the act of laughing together helped you to feel closer to each other. Humorous moments like these can be captured by taking a photo of something related to that incident.

Vacations are traditionally the time when most fathers use cameras to capture and preserve memories. But there are other times and places when photographs can be equally effective to capture memories that you will want to recall. Pictures can be used to communicate changes in your life that would be difficult to describe with words alone, and they can do so more quickly. For instance, if you move, you could send a child a photo of her new room. And photos can build anticipation of an event, such as a vacation, that you're planning with your kids. Use your imagination, and let the examples in this chapter prod your creative thoughts.

TIP 59 | Keep a Photo Album

A collection of pictures can bring back good memories and keep them fresh.

Take photographs during your visits and then compile them into a photo album that you update together. Occasionally bring out the photo album and look back through it with your kids, reminiscing about your adventures and experiences. Always have double sets of pictures developed so that you can give your children a set. Although you might put the first set in a photo album that they could keep updating, kids often do not follow through with this. But they will probably show the pictures to their friends and discuss your time together. The continuity and history of your relationship will be captured in the comprehensive photo album you keep. Be sure to record the date and place of each set of pictures.

An alternate approach would be to expand the photo album into a scrapbook. In the scrapbook, you could not only keep photographs, but also memorabilia from your times spent with your children. You might include restaurant menus that remind you and your kids of a great vacation, ticket stubs to a ball game or a concert, as well as the pictures that go with each event. Altogether, it will provide a fun way to take both you and your children back to the original moments in which you were having fun, sharing excitement, or just enjoying being together.

JOEY ALWAYS TOOK A NUMBER OF PICTURES *during his son Alex's visits, and then he gave Alex a set and put the other set in his own photo album. He tried to capture a variety of interesting images, scenes, and activities that would help to remind Alex of their time together. Sometimes when Alex returned home, he put the photos in a drawer and forgot about them. But occasionally, when Alex was looking for something he couldn't find, he came across the set of pictures in his dresser drawer. Then he would have the fun of remembering the visit and what he and his Dad had experienced together. There were always some pictures that made Alex smile.*

TIP 60 | Take a Photography Class Together

Learning together about photography can nourish creativity in both you and your children.

If you have a camera, show your kids how to use it. And if you have some knowledge about photography, you might teach your children some of the fundamentals. Taking a photography class together is another option. If a child shows enough interest, you could buy her a camera, either regular or digital.

A digital camera will have the advantage of producing pictures that can be uploaded directly from the camera to a computer. The computer can then print out the images on a printer using the appropriate paper. This approach has the advantage of avoiding the cost of film development, plus the digital images could easily be emailed from one computer to another.

Encourage your children to send you pictures of the events and people in their lives. Many kids like to take informal pictures of their friends, and viewing these photographs can help dads to know more about their children.

 KURT WAS A SEVENTEEN-YEAR-OLD *with a love of computers. He also liked the digital camera that his dad, Tom, had given him as a birthday present. When Kurt made a dramatic improvement on his report card, Tom surprised Kurt by taking him to a local computer training center. There they both took a digital photography class that taught*

them how to edit digital photo images on a computer by using editing software. Attending the class with his dad gave Kurt confidence to learn this new skill. Kurt was able to use this new knowledge to contribute to his high school's web site as well as to send pictures to his dad.

TIP 61

Use a PC Camera

Using live video while talking on the telephone adds to the feeling of being together.

One of the wonders of computer technology is the capacity of the most recent computers to show good quality video images. Coupled with a small digital camera mounted on the computer monitor, this is enough to allow two people to see each other while talking on a telephone. With the innovation, it's possible for you to see a child while talking to her. This ability opens up a new channel of communication between you, because you can see the child's body language in addition to hearing the words and the voice. Each of you will be able to see each other's facial expressions, and that will make communicating easier.

When you can see the person you're talking with, the connection feels deeper. The visual feedback allows information to be conveyed which may be difficult to express in words alone. While the technology is constantly evolving, PC cameras have become widely available, and they make it easy for you and your kids to see each other during phone conversations.

What Will It Take to See Your Child?

What you need is one of the commercially available packages that include the PC camera and the software that goes with it. Some of the brands include a portable digital video camera that doubles as a digital still-photography camera. You can get the most inexpensive PC cameras for less than $50. However, if you want the video to be two-way, you'll need two of them (one for each computer). The images have been a bit jerky up until now, but ever-evolving computer technology is improving the quality of this medium dramatically.

TIP 62

Send a Photo Mug

Your kids will have good feelings every time they drink from the photo mugs that you gave them.

Pick a photo of a child doing something well and have it put on a mug. The photo could be of a son playing in a school basketball game or a daughter riding a horse. The pictures with the most power to make a child feel good are the ones that give him recognition for something well done. Award ceremonies where a child receives a certificate, medal, or trophy or some other sign of achievement are opportune times to preserve such memories. Reminding your kids of something they do well is a way of boosting their own self-confidence and self-esteem.

Once you have the right picture, a print shop like Kinko's will put the image on a mug for you for a modest cost. Have two mugs made up, one for the child and one for yourself. Then send a mug to the child with a note like "I'm glad you're my son. Love Dad." When your child visits you, he'll be pleased and proud to see you using the photo mug that you kept for yourself.

JASON WENT TO SEE HIS DAUGHTER MANDY *in a school play. It was the first time she had ever been in a play, and she was quite nervous before the performance. But Mandy remembered her lines perfectly and even received extra applause from the audience at the end of the performance. Using a telephoto lens, Jason got a good shot of her as she took her bow. She had a big grin on her face. Jason had the picture put on a mug and gave it to Mandy on her next visit. His daughter was delighted! She took the mug home and used it every day for months. It meant several things to her. First, it reminded her of the effort she had put into memorizing her lines in the play. Second, it reminded her of the good response she had gotten from the audience which validated her hard work. But the most cherished memory Mandy would recall was the big hug she had gotten from her dad after the show when he whispered into her ear, "I'm proud of you, honey."*

TIP 63 | **Give a T-Shirt with a Selected Photo on It**

Giving your kids a means of showing the world a key event can bolster their self-esteem.

T-shirts naturally attract attention, especially if there are unusual images or messages on them. A picture of a child doing something special, particularly an activity she does well, will remind her of the area she excels in. And that reminder will help her tackle other things. By giving your child a photograph of herself at a time when she is excelling, you're helping her to anchor the image of being successful. And you will amplify this effect when you put the image on a T-shirt.

If you place a caption under the photograph, you can enhance the effect still further. For example, you could use "Champion," "Winner's Circle," or "Heart of a Lion" as a caption on the shirt. Then give it to her and see her face light up. The child will like the fact that you gave her the T-shirt because it shows you care. This gift also says that you are proud of her, and that you want to share your pride with the world. It will make her feel appreciated by you.

Once she's wearing this T-shirt, the child will be even more aware of the image and its associated success. People she encounters throughout the day are likely to comment on the shirt. These experiences will help her own her success out in the world.

DAN AND HIS TWELVE-YEAR-OLD DAUGHTER *Jennifer went on a deep sea fishing trip in the Gulf of Mexico. It was the first time Jennifer had been on such a trip, and she didn't know what to expect. When the boat captain found a school of snapper, he dropped anchor, and Jennifer and her dad began to cast their fishing lines. Immediately Jennifer hooked a six-pound snapper and, after quite a struggle, finally reeled it in. Dan got a good picture of Jennifer grinning broadly at him while holding up her first catch. She was very proud. Dan had the image put on a T-shirt the following week and mailed it to his daughter. Jennifer was thrilled. She began wearing it at every opportunity. People who saw the T-shirt commented on it, and Jennifer never tired of telling her story.*

TIP 64 | Have a Picture Made into a Poster

An image blown up large as life can add immeasurably to your children's memories of their good times with you.

Photographs can be blown up into any size by your local print shop. Try making a poster of a photo from some event when you and a child were together having fun. The association of seeing that poster repeatedly will bring back the good memories of that time to the child. Kids love to hang posters in their rooms, so this can make a fun gift.

If you want to go one step further, framed posters can look very impressive. You might want to buy an inexpensive poster frame at a discount store, such as Wal-Mart, and present the child with a framed poster for his bedroom.

 KEVIN TOOK HIS SON SETH TO A FRIEND'S HOUSE *so the youngster could feed and pet some horses. Seth's French bulldog, Jonah, accompanied them. Seth began feeding the horses the carrots he had brought with him. Suddenly Jonah lunged with great gusto at all the carrots that had fallen on the ground, eating every one he could reach. They all laughed at the dog's enthusiasm for eating the carrots. Kevin later used a photo of Seth, the horses, and Jonah to make a large poster. He sent it to his son and Seth hung it on a wall in his room. The poster reminded Seth of the fun time he had with his dad. When Seth's friends asked him about the poster, he enjoyed telling them about feeding the horses and about laughing with his dad at Jonah.*

TIP 65 | Share Pictures from Your Life

Meaningful images from your current life will give your kids a way of understanding you.

Pictures tell stories in a different way than words alone. That's why one picture can mean so much to a child. By sending the child photographs of significant things that are happening in your life, you're revealing the parts of yourself that will allow your child to get to know you.

As changes take place in your life, take photographs and send them to your kids. For example, if you move to a different place, send pictures, being sure to include photos of the children's new rooms. If you get a new pet or a new car, send pictures. If you paint the outside of your house a different color or plant new trees, send pictures. This will help your kids to visualize and anchor the changes that have taken place in between their visits.

 WHEN KEVIN DECIDED TO GET A PUPPY *to keep his older dog company, he immediately sent pictures of the Irish setter to his daughter Alicia. During their phone conversations, Kevin shared all of the "new puppy" stories with Alicia, but he also followed up by sending pictures of some of the funny things the Irish setter was doing. Alicia started to feel an interest in and connection to the puppy long before she actually got to see it in person. She also took pictures to school and showed them to friends and teachers, sharing the excitement about her father's pet.*

TIP 66 | Build Anticipation with Photos

Get your kids excited about being with you by sending fun pictures beforehand.

You can whet your children's appetite for seeing you by sending pictures. If you have a special activity planned for a visit, send a picture beforehand of something connected with the activity.

For example, let's say a child will be playing on a softball team during his summer stay with you. You could take a picture of a new softball and mitt sitting on the dresser in his bedroom and send the photo to him some weeks prior to the visit. A visual image reinforces what you have told a child and makes it more real.

Maybe you have bought new fishing poles or new snow sleds that you are looking forward to using with your children. Sending photos before your next visit with the kids will build anticipation as they look forward to trying out the new equipment.

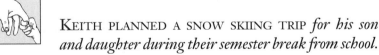

KEITH PLANNED A SNOW SKIING TRIP *for his son and daughter during their semester break from school. Prior to the trip, he sent pictures of the colorful ski outfits and warm caps and gloves he had bought for them. Keith planned to rent their ski equipment, so he could not send pictures of the actual skis. Instead, he found magazine pictures of skiers that he cut out and included in his letter. As Keith's children looked at the pictures, the ski trip seemed even more real than it had previously. They started to look forward with excitement to their upcoming adventure.*

❖ ❖ ❖

Laughing with your kids makes up for
a lot of tears.

CHAPTER 9

Enjoy Recreational Activities: Explore Fun Things

Having fun together should be an important part of your relationship with your kids. Without fun, there won't be many good memories to share and treasure. How are you currently having fun with your children? You may have discovered that finding ways to have fun with them can sometimes be a challenge. It could require taking a risk to try something new. Risks, by definition, involve taking a chance that something may not work the way you wanted or expected. But you may also find an experience that can provide rich memories in future years.

What you discover to be fun for your kids may vary

127

from the experiences of other fathers. Try using the suggestions in this chapter as guidelines to help you explore a variety of activities until you find the right mix. Throughout your kids' childhood, you'll want to use bonding opportunities well. When a child is young, reading bedtime stories and spending uninterrupted time together are good ways to bond. As the child grows older, you will find that more active endeavors—like learning new skills together, going places, or playing games—or creative activities such as making things will produce long-lasting positive memories. More passive activities like playing computer games or watching television will make less of an impact on your bonding with the children.

Also, remember that the interests of kids can change over time. So don't assume that they will always like to do the same things. When children enter the teenage years, they tend to reevaluate their priorities and redefine for themselves what they like to do. It takes creativity and flexibility to find new ways of connecting with a child when the former methods aren't working. Sometimes, the only change that is needed is to allow a child to ask a friend to come along and to participate in the activities you have planned. It's a wise father who can "go with the flow" and allow his children to change what they like without trying to make them feel guilty.

TIP 67 | Learn a Useful Skill Together

By learning together, you can gain new knowledge while deepening your bond with a child.

Did you ever want to learn something new, but never took the time to do it? If it's something that a son or daughter would also enjoy, try learning about it together. Are you into crafts? How about gardening? Would you benefit by learning new computer skills? There are plenty of skills to choose from that could be useful to you and the child.

There are many community learning outlets scattered across the U.S. Sometimes they are privately owned businesses, like computer training centers with a terminal for each student. Public schools and colleges offer community classes on such diverse subjects as automotive repair, gourmet cooking, music, art, foreign languages, or drama. Local art museums in some cities sponsor weekend classes designed for parents and their elementary-aged kids to learn paper-mache modeling, kite building, or other creative skills.

For many fathers, the best time to schedule such learning opportunities is during the summer visitation, when kids may stay for a month or longer. Using part of this time to learn a new skill together can help to strengthen your relationship in a lasting way.

PETE LIKED TO DRAW WHEN HE WAS A KID. *However by the time he was in high school, Pete was into sports more than anything else. His parents divorced when Pete was in the tenth grade, and sports probably saved him from getting into trouble. Then in the summer between his junior and senior years of high school, Pete's dad suggested they take a mechanical drawing class together at the local community college. It turned out to lead to something good for both of them. Pete enrolled at the University of Michigan and majored in mechanical engineering, and his father used the experience in a change of careers. Pete feels that taking the class together that summer also helped him and his dad find a good reason to spend time together. Now they have an interest they can share for years to come.*

TIP 68 — Play Interactive Internet Games

Getting involved together in an ongoing online game gives you a reason to stay in touch.

If you and your kids like games, there's a way to play against each other even if you live a distance away from your children. Many game web sites allow you to play with one or more people at the same time. A number of hyperlinks to game web sites are found at Yahoo.com. A quick glance at the kids' section there will show you dozens of games that are available and that you can play interactively with your kids. You can either play in real time or else with delayed responses. A game could last just one session, or it can stretch out over days or even weeks. Most of the links go to games that are free to play, although some may involve the purchase of a CD Rom for a modest charge from the game web site.

You can add to the suspense of who will win a particular game by requiring the losers to do something for the winner. Yet remember to keep the competition light without getting too caught up in who will win, so that you'll all have more fun. As always, keep in mind that your purpose is to use interactive games to bond with your kids. Any other goal may be counterproductive to maintaining a healthy and balanced relationship with your children.

3 Qualities of a Useful Game Web Site

There are thousands of web sites related to games. Sites that will meet your needs for staying connected to your kids should be:

1. **Child-appropriate**—The site features games and content that are right for you and the kids.

2. **Interactive**—Two or more players who are distant from each other can play in the same game.

3. **Multi-session**—You'll have the capability of extending the play of a game over more than one session.

TIP 69 | Learn a Sport Together

By encouraging your children to exercise, you can help establish habits that will keep them active and healthy.

Exercise is a necessity for anyone who wants to maintain good health throughout a long life. And since health is so important, you can give your children something precious by helping them to develop the habit of exercising on a regular basis. Encouraging an interest in a sport is one way to do this.

Learning a sport that you can pursue on vacations and visits can give you yet another opportunity to bond with your kids. Some sports to consider are kayaking, water skiing, tennis, golf, archery, canoeing, rappelling, snow skiing, sailing, hiking, backpacking, scuba diving, roller blading, lifting weights, swimming, or mountain biking.

If you're initially clumsy in your attempts to master a new sport, don't be embarrassed that your kids are seeing you struggle. It's helpful for children to see their dads experience the role of a beginner learning a new skill. That way, they don't feel badly themselves when struggling to learn something new. This is a good opportunity for you to be a positive role model. If you can learn to laugh at yourself while learning, it's all the better. You'll be teaching your kids that they don't always have to be perfect when they try something new.

DENNIS HAD ALWAYS THOUGHT THAT HE HAD TO BE PERFECT *when doing anything, and that otherwise his parents would not approve. He even blamed himself for his parents' divorce because Dennis was the subject of many of their fights. Dennis started to obsess about doing everything perfectly. He thought that he had to make straight A's, be the most popular kid in school, and excel in sports. Dennis hesitated to do things in front of other people that he couldn't do well because they might think less of him. Much to his surprise, when Dennis was in the eighth grade, his dad suggested that they learn to sail. So during spring break, they spent a week in Florida taking sailing lessons. Dennis caught on rather quickly, but his dad, who had never been sailing before, was a real klutz. Never having seen him when he wasn't "Mr. Competent," this came as a shock to Dennis. His dad kept getting the sailing terms mixed up, he couldn't tie most of the sailor's knots, and his attempts to "come about" and adjust the sails were embarrassing. But what amazed Dennis was that in spite of everything, his father still said that he was having a good time! Dennis thought his dad would say that he hated it. But when Dennis' father goofed up, he'd just laugh and say that he was glad that at least one of them was catching on. After that summer, Dennis finally felt much less pressure to be perfect.*

TIP 70 | **Help a Child Start a Collection**

By collecting, your kids will develop curiosity to learn more about their areas of interest.

Collections give dads and their kids ample opportunities to bond. When you're together, start a collection of something that interests a child. Take coin collecting, for instance. Coins introduce kids to the political figures whose images are featured on them. Coins also introduce children to national symbols like the bald eagle, and they teach kids financial value. A child might choose to collect U.S. coins, or she might want to collect foreign coins. Collecting stamps offers similar learning experiences for kids.

Any type of collection a child chooses can lead to learning opportunities. Collecting shells can set the stage for a lesson in marine biology. A collection of comic books might teach the child about graphic design. A collection of rocks could stir an interest in geology. If you help the child with her collection, you will have stimulated her mind with something besides television or video games.

Help the child to start her collection and to figure out how to organize it. If she needs a coin collector's album, provide the first one for her. If she wants to collect stamps, buy her some stamps to help her get started, along with a stamp collector's album. Other items to collect are baseball cards, Beanie Babies, model planes, miniature cars, or Barbie dolls. Whatever your child chooses, occasionally send her another item to add to her collection and help the child learn more about this area of interest. Collections will increase your chances to teach and to motivate your children to learn. In the process, you are supporting your kids' interests and increasing the closeness between you.

WHEN JIMMY WAS ABOUT TEN, *his dad brought home a stamp collection kit. Afterwards the two of them spent many enjoyable hours together pasting in stamps and discussing them. Stamps helped Jimmy learn about the countries of the world. They led to geography lessons about where the countries are located. And pictures on the stamps provided clues about the politics in each country. Jimmy learned something about world events and history, just through a simple stamp collection.*

TIP 71 | Cook Favorite Recipes

If you cook, share your knowledge with your kids.

During visits, teach your children to cook their favorite foods and your special family recipes. Make copies of the recipe for your kids, and ask them to let you know how the food turns out when they make it themselves later.

Let your kids know that having recipes "bomb out" is part of the process of cooking. Advise them that when this happens, they should analyze what went wrong so they can learn from the experience. If a recipe "bombs out" during one of your cooking sessions together, find whatever is funny about it, laugh together, and then go out for pizza!

HOWARD TAUGHT HIS SON MARK TO COOK *several of his favorite foods during the time they spent together in the summer. By the end of the visitation, Mark knew how to make grilled cheese sandwiches, pancakes, stuffed baked potatoes, and his father's top-secret barbecue sauce. After Mark returned home, he was able to impress his friends and family by offering to cook these foods. Each time, Mark would proudly state, "My Dad taught me how to do this." Mark looked for opportunities to show off his new abilities and to tell the story of how his father taught him to cook. Years later, Mark still enjoyed making the barbecue sauce and announcing to his friends that it was a "top-secret family recipe" his dad had shared with him.*

4 Tips on Teaching Your Kids Cooking Skills

1. **Always make sure that safety rules are followed in the kitchen.** Utensils like knives and electric appliances like toasters and microwave ovens have safety guidelines that must be followed. Make sure your children know what these guidelines are.

2. **Start with easy things first.** Specialty sandwiches and fruit smoothies are simple to master and easy to teach your children.

3. **Consider purchasing a cookbook written for children or teens, depending on the age of your kids.** Make sure that the instructions are simple and that the recipes are illustrated with numerous color pictures.

4. **Don't forget to encourage good nutrition.** Balance your children's diet when they are with you, and teach them to eat a healthy variety of foods.

Try Bird Watching

Encouraging bird watching teaches kids about nature's diversity and the environment.

You can enrich your children's knowledge about nature by watching birds with them. The vast diversity of winged creatures provide a fascinating means of provoking a child's curiosity. Think for a moment of where birds like to build nests or search for insects in your neighborhood. Perhaps there is a city park nearby with a lot of trees where birds build nests. Or there could be a patch of woods down the street from your house in which an abundance of crawly things are available for birds to eat. These would be good places to watch birds.

Give your children a pair of binoculars and encourage them to keep watching birds when they are not with you. Encourage them to get books on birds out of the library. You might ask a child to find out a particular piece of information. If you have sparrows in your back yard, ask him to find out where sparrows migrate in the winter. If he discovers that some birds that live near you migrate to South America in the winter, the child will have learned something new. Ask the right questions of your kids and you will expand their awareness of the world around them.

Study bird watching with your children and tell them to keep a list of what they see when you're not together. You keep a list too. Then compare notes when you talk by phone or visit with the kids in person. If your community has a local Audubon Society, arrange for you and your kids to accompany them on a bird-watching expedition one weekend.

WHEN ROBERTA WAS ABOUT FIVE, *her dad was living in an apartment on the second floor of an older building. The bathroom had a window that looked toward an alley. There, on the window sill, a family of pigeons built a nest. Roberta's dad had pointed out the nest to his daughter and encouraged her to watch the birds. Roberta was excited about the nest every time she visited her dad. She could check out the pigeons any time she wanted by standing on a chair and peeking over the edge of the window frame. At first, Roberta would scare away the mother that was sitting on the nest, but then she found a way to peek through the curtains so the bird wouldn't startle. When two of the eggs hatched, Roberta was amazed to watch the chicks get fed every day for a while. Then suddenly, they were gone. To this day, she has a curiosity about birds that started with that experience.*

TIP 73 | Make Up Songs or Poems

Customizing existing songs with your own words can be a fun activity to share with the kids.

Most kids like music, songs, and poems. Even young children usually enjoy catchy tunes and songs written for kids their age. You can encourage your children's love of music by buying them a recording of kids' music and then singing along with them as it is played. Once they are familiar with the songs, try to vary them by making up new words. You might include a child's or pet's name in the new lyrics.

Do you have a special song that you sing whenever you are together or that perhaps you sing at bedtime? Record yourself singing the song and send the tape to your kids.

During a visit, ask your children to help you make up a funny song, then make a tape of all of you singing it together. You could send the tape home with your kids at the end of the visit. Sing or "serenade" your children when you call them on the phone.

You can also make up a poem together. Email a child the first line of a poem you are starting to write and ask him to write the next line and send it back to you. Alternate writing the lines until the poem feels finished. When the poem is completed, send the child a copy of the finished version.

A FATHER WE KNOW WROTE THE LINE "I LOVE TO FISH" *and emailed it to his son. His son wrote the second line, "And I have just one wish." They alternated creating lines back and forth, coming up with this poem:*

> *I love to fish*
> *And I have just one wish.*
> *It's to catch a really big one*
> *And to have lots of fun.*

TIP 74 | Read or Create Stories

Fantasy tales are one of the best ways to provoke a child's imagination.

Reading bedtime stories to young children is a wonderful way to bond with them. A child will love it when you do this. She gets to sit close to you as the two of you look at the book together. As you look at the illustrations, ask her questions that will make her an active participant instead of just a passive observer. "How many cats are in this picture?" or "Can you point to the giraffe?" are questions that you might ask a young child. Challenge the child to think as you read the book to her. Ask her what she thinks will happen next or how the story might be changed.

Older children may enjoy listening to age-appropriate books on tape as you ride in the car together or at your house. That way, you are hearing the same thing and can discuss your reactions to the story as you go along.

For older kids, email a child the first sentence of a very short story. In the story, the child might be the protagonist. Ask her to write the next sentence and send it back to you. Alternate writing the sentences until you have filled up a page and one of you writes, "The End." When the story is finished, send the child a copy of the completed version. If you know how to use computer graphics, add pictures. If the finished product is a story that the child really likes, make an audiotape of your reading of it.

A FATHER WE KNOW SENT HIS DAUGHTER *an email of the beginning of a story. The line read: "It was early morning when the dinosaur egg cracked open." His daughter wrote the second sentence, "The baby dinosaur was named Rex." The father responded, "Rex was very hungry and decided to look for food." His daughter wrote, "Then he got into trouble." The father added, "A huge bird with a long sharp beak saw Rex and started coming after him." The daughter ended with, "But Rex hid in the woods and he was okay. The End."*

| TIP 75 | **Plant a Garden** |

Growing vegetables or flowers together can help you connect with your kids.

A vegetable or flower garden can encourage an interest in nature in general, or in plants in particular. Growing a garden introduces your children to the life cycle of plants and to the seasons. Your kids will learn when and how to water the plants, fertilize them, and otherwise take care of the garden. This will provide you and the kids time together outside in nature. You can talk with them as you all work. Bonding is promoted when you're involved in a joint project together and share mutual pride in the outcome.

If you can, plant your garden with your children during a visitation time. If this is not possible, you can plant it and then send pictures of the garden to your kids. When they come to visit, the children will see how much the plants have grown. They can help to take care of the garden during their stay. When any vegetables are ready to pick, they can help. They'll enjoy eating what they have helped to grow. The kids will also like taking some of the vegetables or flowers back to their mom to show her what they have accomplished. Also take pictures of the garden and mail them to your children after they go back to their mom's house. Or you could take some vegetables with you if you visit the children during the growing season.

AS A KID, HEATHER NEVER WANTED TO EAT *many vegetables. Her mom had always tried to convince her to eat them but the little girl was stubborn. Then, in late spring during one of her visits, Heather's dad suggested that she plant a few lima beans in his garden. She got excited when her father told her on the phone a few days later that the first sprouts had come up. Heather's father helped tend the plants between visitations and he kept her informed as the plants matured. That summer, Heather watched the plants grow every day when she stayed with her dad for a month. As the pods took shape, she began to imagine how the beans might taste. Finally the big day arrived! Heather harvested her tiny crop and gave them to her father to cook for supper. She stared at the fourteen beans on her plate for a long time. Then, for the first time in Heather's life, she ate lima beans! Before this time, she had hated them. But now Heather liked lima beans because of all the trouble she had gone to in order to grow her first crop. Later she liked more and more vegetables. But the real gift was the fun she had with her dad in watching the plants grow for weeks.*

TIP 76 | Research Your Family Tree

If you encourage an interest in your ancestral lineage, you give your kids a sense of history and your family's place in it.

Perhaps you don't know much about your family's history. This will not present a problem if you decide you want to learn something about your heritage. There are a number of web sites that will allow you to research your family name. Also, public libraries have resources that can help you trace your ancestral roots.

Take your kids to visit some of the older relatives in your family who know more of the family history than you do. Ask them to share stories and pictures with your children. Also, talk with your kids about what nationality your last name represents and how your ancestors probably came to America.

ON ONE RECENT VISIT THAT KATIE MADE *to her dad's home, he took her to visit his grandmother, a sharp lady of ninety-nine years who still lived alone. At one point, her father discovered a drawer full of old photographs in the grandmother's house. "What are these?" he asked his grandmother. She proceeded to tell Katie and her dad that the photos were of their family, dating back to the early twentieth century. Katie got to hear firsthand stories of her great grandmother's childhood, of people using horses and buggies, and of the first telephone in the small town where the grandmother lived. She got to see those old yellowing photos of part of her family's history and to imagine how life was back then. Katie learned how the number of ancestors that one has multiplies by two with every generation that is traced back in time. She saw a picture of her great, great, great grandmother, dressed like a hillbilly from West Virginia. And Katie got a sense of the family's general character, of what they were generations ago. This meant a lot to both Katie and her dad. It bonded them together with a common ancestral line.*

TIP 77 | Learn about Foreign Places Together

Reading to your children about foreign places and cultures is a good way to teach them about the world.

If a child is very young and you still read stories to her at bedtime, occasionally choose books that depict foreign lands. If you would like her to understand and appreciate her own heritage, choose some books related to countries where your ancestors lived. You don't have to know the specific details of your own family, although if you have that information, it would add interest.

Teach your kids to be curious about the world by learning words and phrases from other countries. Broaden their view of the world we live in. Teach the children about how customs vary in different parts of the world. Teach them how some of our customs were derived from foreign cultures. If your budget will allow it, plan a trip to a foreign country. Before you travel, practice saying specific things in the foreign tongue during phone calls.

WHEN LAURA WAS PERHAPS SIX YEARS OLD, *her dad started reading stories to her whenever she would visit him. She liked it when he read the story about Madeline, the little French girl living in a boarding school run by Catholic nuns in Paris. Her dad Ken was insightful enough to point out various elements in the story and illustrations, and this made it more interesting and enjoyable for Laura. She learned that the architecture of buildings in France is different from the U.S. Laura's dad also pointed out some of the differences in food, such as the long loaves of French bread shown in the book. She learned that a word in their language, "oui," sounds like "we" in English and means yes. That experience of her father reading books like this to Laura at a young age sowed the seeds of her later interest in foreign affairs.*

Prepare your kids for the future by giving them a world view of our global community.

| TIP 78 | **Plant Something on Special Occasions** |

Planting a tree in honor of a child at a special time in his life will remind him of your support for years to come.

One way to recognize and celebrate a child's major accomplishments and significant events is to plant something that will be likely to grow and thrive for years to come, such as a tree. This symbol of the child's efforts will grow bigger and taller each year, reminding him of the achievement and your support.

Occasions that could call for planting a tree include the child's baptism, confirmation, bar or bat mitzvah, graduation from elementary or middle school, or graduation from high school or college. Other times to consider would be when a child receives an outstanding honor or recognition that will be meaningful for the rest of his life.

JOHNNY BECAME A BOY SCOUT *and earned merit badges rapidly. The week Johnny turned thirteen, he finally achieved the Eagle badge. That weekend, Johnny went to visit his dad Bill. To celebrate the new badge, Bill had bought a small apple tree at a local plant nursery. The father and son planted it together in Bill's backyard. Over the span of several years, it grew into a producer of apples that the two of them would pick. To Johnny, this activity always reminded him of the recognition his dad had given him for his accomplishment. As time passed, the tree grew large, and in Johnny's mind, it was a magnificent symbol of what he could accomplish when he was determined to reach a goal.*

TIP 79 | Broadcast a Radio Dedication

Radio stations that allow song requests give dads a chance to broadcast their esteem and love for their kids to the listening audience.

Music has always had a powerful influence on children, especially teenagers. Most of them have favorite songs, musical groups, and radio stations. One well-known radio format is the call-in show that allows listeners to request a particular song and dedicate it to someone special. By dedicating a song to a child on the radio, you have a chance to surprise her and to announce to the world why you think she is special.

Before doing this, think about how the child might react. Teenagers who are going through the stage of being embarrassed that they even have parents might not appreciate this gesture. Other kids would be thrilled and love hearing their name on the radio.

Gestures like this can mean a lot to your children, and your acts of recognition, encouragement, and support are magnified when you share them with the world. A child can then say, "Yes, I do have a dad who will tell anyone who will listen that he cares about me."

JOHN DECIDED TO TEST THIS METHOD *to surprise his ten-year-old daughter Tessa in recognition for her having done well on a test. He knew that Tessa liked to listen to a particular station while she did her homework. This station allowed call-in requests. One evening when John knew Tessa would be starting to study, he called and told her to listen to the station for something special. Tessa was thrilled when the radio announcer mentioned her by name and played a favorite song in response to a request from "her loving father." Tessa felt that her dad was showing the world that he was proud of her.*

TIP 80 | Tell Your Favorite Stories of Them

You will improve your bond with your children by sharing treasured memories of their early years.

As a parent, you know how cute your kids were as babies. In fact, many parents say that the ages from one to about five years of age have been the source of some of their best memories. Naturally, your children don't remember all those incidents, but you do.

Share your memories of those times with your kids. Maybe there was a time when your son wanted to help do a chore around the house, like raking leaves in the yard. Even though he was too small to handle the rake, he still made a valiant effort. Or remember your daughter on her fourth birthday when she wanted to cut the cake? You had to help guide her hand as she cut her own piece, but she was very proud of herself afterwards.

Your children will enjoy hearing you speak of these precious memories and stories from their early childhood. They will appreciate it if you talk about how cute, funny, or smart they are.

WHEN CHRISTIE WAS THREE AND HER DAD *was still married to her mom, they used to drive for five hours to visit a relative. Naturally, since Christie was so young, she had to sit in a child's seat, located on the back seat of the car. Christie didn't like being alone by herself while Jerry and Lisa sat up front, and soon she would start crying. The only way Jerry found that would make Christie stop was to sing to her. He is not a great singer, but Christie seemed to like it. So, for the entire trip—five hours going up, and five hours coming back home—Jerry would sing every song he had ever heard or knew, over and over. If he would momentarily stop, Christie would cry out, "More, more." Now that Christie is a teenager, she laughs when her dad reminds her of this scenario from over a decade earlier. That memory is one more thing that bonds them together.*

A thoughtfully chosen present, even if it's inexpensive, can have more impact on your child than a flashy gift bought on impulse.

CHAPTER 10

Splurge Occasionally: Send Gifts That Say You Care

Some dads go overboard in buying their kids gifts. They may do so out of a sense of guilt, as if to say, "I can't be there for you as I would like to be, but at least I can compensate by buying you a lot of stuff."

While kids *do* like to receive material gifts, the gift of your heartfelt love will ultimately mean more. Giving consistently and generously of your time and energy is much more important than giving gifts of toys, games, or clothes. Nevertheless, in our society, giving things is a way of life. While giving gifts should not be the core of your strategy in bonding with your children, you will want to offer presents on special occasions like birthdays and on holidays such as Christmas or other seasonal celebrations.

Kids benefit when dads can keep a healthy perspective and a good balance about gift giving. Either extreme—either giving no gifts at all or giving an excess of gifts—is not helpful to your relationship with your children.

Your gifts to your kids do not necessarily have to be expensive to make the point that you care for them. Surprising children with small, inexpensive, unexpected gifts that show you're aware of their interests and wishes can often have a more positive impact on your relationship than more expensive gifts at expected times.

Many fathers try to buy their kids' affection without putting in the necessary effort to connect at an emotional level. If giving gifts is your primary way of showing your kids that you love them, your relationship will be superficial and lacking in intimacy. Balance is the key.

TIP 81 | Provide Gift Certificates or Coupons

Even without knowing exactly what a child likes, you can make the perfect gift.

Perhaps you know that a child likes music but you're not sure which groups are popular right now. One solution is to ask a local music store if they offer gift certificates. If the child lives a long distance from you, inquire at a regional or national chain store about vouchers that you can send that would be redeemable at her local branch.

You could make your own coupons to reward a child for a certain behavior or performance. For example, you may decide that every time the child brings home good grades from school she gets a signed coupon from you worth X dollars. In a set time—such as the end of each month, or when the next report card arrives—she may redeem all of her coupons for cash from you. The coupon might look like this:

This coupon entitles _____
to $_____ worth of merchandise in any
store in recognition of good work.
*Signed:*_____

This simple template graphic can be produced using basic functions found in Microsoft Word. Or else, you may just create one by hand with the same information on it. You could also make a copy of it from this book and fill in the blanks. Use a pen with blue ink to sign your name to distinguish an original copy.

TIP 82 · Buy a Music CD or Tape

A special musical reminder of an event can prompt a child's favorable recollection of her time with you.

Music has a way of stirring emotions. That's why it's used so effectively in movies to amplify the impact of a particular scene. Similarly, when you and a child listen to the same music and enjoy it together, it tends to amplify a shared feeling of connection between you.

When a child is visiting you, you can establish and reinforce a bond based on your common appreciation of a particular song, soundtrack, or artist. When you go to a special event where music is playing, it may have a similar anchoring effect that will increase the pleasure of the moment.

To have the maximum impact, notice what music the child likes that she has heard when the two of you were together. Then give a CD of the music you have both enjoyed. A soundtrack of a play or movie that the two of you saw could bring back wonderful memories for her of being with you each time she plays it.

Perhaps you took your son to a football game and noticed that he liked the song "We Will Rock You" when it was played over the loudspeaker system. Or maybe you took your daughter to see the *Nutcracker*, and she told you that she liked the music. Be aware of a child's mood when music is playing, and you'll more easily key into what the child likes. And, of course, just asking, "Do you like this music?" could give you the feedback you need.

DEAN TOOK HIS DAUGHTER CARMEN *to see "The Music Man" in New York City the week after Christmas. She was fourteen at the time. This was her first exposure to a Broadway musical production, and they were both excited. It was also special for them because the trip was the first Dean had taken her on out of state. Later, when it was close to the time for them to part, he gave her the soundtrack of the play. Dean knew that it had a special meaning to Carmen when she later told him about playing it at home. The music brought back a flood of memories reminding Carmen of the pleasurable time they had together.*

TIP 83 | Send Flowers or Plants

An unexpected gift can delight your kids.

Send a child a special plant or a bouquet of flowers. Boys might enjoy having a cactus plant or bonsai tree to observe, while girls may enjoy receiving a bouquet of roses or assorted spring flowers to display in a vase.

In some junior high and high schools, girls who are participating in school beauty pageants or talent shows often receive a dozen roses from their parents. Local florists usually deliver the flowers to the school on the day of the pageant or the day before if it falls on a weekend. When Nancy was a school counselor in a school where this was the custom, she learned that it was really important to the girls to receive the flowers at school in front of their friends and peers. If the flowers had been sent to their homes instead, the impact would not have been the same. Flowers were also sometimes sent if a girl was participating in homecoming or some other significant school event. This custom will vary from school to school, so check with your child's principal or school counselor to learn what's accepted in their environment.

If you give a live plant, be sure to tell the child how to take care of it. If you're not sure, ask for instructions at the store when you buy or order it. Many plants come with instruction cards that give recommendations about sunlight and watering. Giving a child a plant to care for can provide an educational experience as well as the spark of desire to learn more.

WHEN TOM TOOK HIS SON REGGIE *to the local botanical gardens, Reggie was fascinated by the bonsai displays. A few weeks later, right before one of Reggie's visits, Tom noticed some bonsai trees for sale at a grocery store. Tom decided to buy one for Reggie and surprise him with it during the next visit. Reggie took the bonsai tree home with him and kept it alive for several years. Whenever Tom would come across new information about bonsai, he would send it to Reggie. One weekend when Reggie visited, Tom took him to hear a guest speaker give a short presentation on bonsai gardening at the botanical gardens. Tom then became more interested in bonsai and bought himself a bonsai tree. This delighted Reggie and created some competition between them as to who could care best for his tree.*

TIP 84 | Select a Book of a Particular Genre

A targeted book about a child's special interest is likely to be read and appreciated.

Books are the gateway to learning. They can also be a way to stir a child's imagination. If properly presented to a child, books can offer a world of benefits, of stimulation, and of knowledge. You can do a child a big favor by helping him to cultivate the habit of reading about things he's interested in.

Teach your kids the benefits of learning through reading. Many books for children offer elements of fantasy.

Thus, like video games or television, they can serve as escapes. But reading is superior to many other ways a child can spend his time because it is active, not passive. Unlike other popular pastimes, reading forces a child to use his mind and prepares him for the real world where learning and knowledge is valued.

If you have a preschool child, you might send an age-appropriate storybook with an accompanying tape of you reading the story. If the child cannot read, you can make a special sound on the tape to indicate when it's time for him to turn the page. If there's a puppet that could go along with the story, send it along with the book and tape.

Another variation is to start reading the new book to a child during a visit and then record the tape before he leaves to go home, sending it with him. If you've been making the story come alive by using a puppet, send it home with him too.

ALLEN'S THIRTEEN-YEAR-OLD SON SAM LIKES CATS. *Sam grew up with a gray tabby cat, Maxwell, at his mom's house, but recently the cat died. Sam was really down. He had adored Maxwell. At a bookstore, Allen found a book that featured heart-tugging stories of people and their pets. It was called "Chicken Soup for the Animal Lover's Soul." Allen gave it to Sam and didn't hear anything about it for a week. Then, one evening Sam called his father unexpectedly and said, "Dad, thanks for giving me that book. It meant a lot. It helped me understand that other people have feelings about their pets just like I did."*

Buy a Share of Stock

TIP 85

Giving your kids stock as a gift will provide them with a lesson about economics.

In our world today, few other social forces shape the way we live as much as the economy. You can help your children by teaching them something about the way our economic system works. You might start by making an investment in their future by buying them one or more shares of stock in a publicly traded company.

If you're not very knowledgeable about stocks, this could be a great opportunity to learn so that you can then teach your children the fundamentals. At the same time, you would be gaining knowledge that can help you in planning for the security of both yourself and your kids.

By giving your children shares of a company that you personally have an interest in, you might make it more fun. Make sure, however, that if you have a large investment in a company that decreases in value, it does not negatively impact your mood when you're around the children. It may be wise to buy them a few shares of stock in a company that you like but are not heavily invested in yourself. That way, you avoid having emotional stress between you and your kids if the stock goes down.

The point is not necessarily to make money in the children's accounts, although that would be nice. Instead you can think of the experience as an opportunity to teach your kids (and perhaps also learn something yourself) about how a company's activities and the economy at large affect the price of stocks.

A Tip on Buying Stocks

Go to www.oneshare.com in order to purchase one share of stock from your choice of a range of companies. There you will find stock tips and instructions on how to make a gift of corporate equity that will last and (hopefully) grow in value instead of a gift that will simply be used up or wear out. The site gives advice and states, "Teach your children how to be owners, not just consumers. [Our site is] called the most interactive way to teach your children about stock ownership!"

TIP 86 | Customize a Book

You can have a book specially printed with a child's name as the main character.

Small kids are like the rest of us. Whenever something has our name on it, we tend to pay more attention. Due to advances in digital technology, you can now order children's books that are customized to feature the names you choose for the characters. Therefore you can specify a child's name as the main protagonist in the story. You might also name the child's pet (for example, a dog, cat, goldfish, etc.) as an animal to be included too. In addition, you could set the location in your child's town.

This feature will naturally make a child fascinated with the plot of the book. It can help to interest a child in books and to motivate him to read. Before you give the book to him, try building up suspense by saying something like, "I've got a surprise for you to look at. It's about you and Sparky (his dog)." Then read the book to him, perhaps at bedtime. Play with his imagination by stopping several times for questions. You might ask, "What do you think will happen next?" or "Does this picture really look like you?"

If you have more than one child, you can customize a book for each of them. That way, every child will feel special, and they will have a vested interest in how the story in the book unfolds. This can help to stimulate their interest in books and reading.

3 Web Sites on Customizing Books

Several attractive web sites allow you to specify and order customized books. They are listed below. Prices per book are in the $11 range.

1. www.apersonalizedbook.com

2. www.abc123books.com

3. www.mlminterbiz.com/childstarbooks

TIP 87

Purchase Toys and Kits

Take into consideration what toys a child has and consider accessories.

Childhood should be a time of play. These are the formative years when the imagination can be nurtured by healthy stimulation. All kids enjoy receiving toys, games, stuffed animals, or creative play materials such as modeling clay, costumes for playing dress-up, or puppets. A balanced approach to providing a child with these playthings can help him to develop his mind and creativity.

Consider accessories to existing toys or interests that a child currently has. If he owns a bike, perhaps the child would enjoy a bell or horn for it. A child who loves to paint might like to have an easel and a new assortment of tempura paints in a variety of colors.

You can also consider giving the child a kit that contains something to build or make. Kits can be beneficial because they require skill and patience from the child in order to assemble the pieces. Kits also teach kids the names of the components in whatever it is they are putting together. There are a number of educational kits designed for the purpose of stimulating interest in science or nature. And, of course, don't forget traditional kits like model cars and airplanes.

 IN THE SUMMER WHEN JASON WAS ELEVEN, *he visited his father Marty. Jason's dad bought him a model airplane kit to build a motor-driven, miniature propeller airplane. It was the old-fashioned kind made from balsa wood and lacquered paper that was propelled by a small gasoline engine. Marty had built similar models when he was a kid, except this one was radio remote-controlled. He showed his son how to begin, and then got out of Jason's way. It was challenging, but Jason finally got it finished. Jason will never forget the feeling of accomplishment he had when they went to an open field for the plane's first flight. Now Jason feels that doing this project helped him develop persistence. Jason's father showed his son that he could successfully complete something that was hard. It helped Jason believe in his own abilities.*

Order a Magazine Subscription

TIP
88

You can encourage a child to read and pursue his hobbies by providing a subscription to a magazine of interest.

A child's interest could be like the seed of a great apple tree planted in the fertile soil. If properly cultivated, it has a chance to grow into something substantial with branches capable of bearing fruit in the future.

Find out what the child's interests are and help him to cultivate new ones. Does he like to build things? Is he athletic? Does he enjoy being outdoors? Does he like animals? Does he like cars, trucks, or motorcycles? What does he like to collect? Perhaps he gravitates toward creative activities such as drawing or music.

Send the child a magazine subscription based on what you discover about his interests. The beauty of giving a child a magazine is that your gift is spread throughout the year, and he will think of you when each issue arrives. Reading a magazine about an area of interest can broaden his perspective, increase his knowledge, and improve his vocabulary. And it will provide material for the two of you to talk about.

A child's teacher may have some good suggestions about which magazine she feels your child would enjoy the most. Before you place an order, check with your ex-wife to be sure that he's not already receiving the same magazine you have in mind. You may get a few additional ideas from the web sites on the next page.

3 Web Sites of Kids' Magazines

Go to any one of the following web sites to find a selection of children's periodicals.

1. **www.Amazon.com**—Click first in the menu bar on *Magazines*, then *Search*. Then type "kids" in the subject box.

2. **www.Barnesandnoble.com**—Type in "kids' magazines" in the subject box.

3. **www.Magazine.counter.net**—Click on *Children's Magazines*.

Name a Star after a Child

You can make a child feel unique and special with a celestial gift.

Encouragement is the best way to help a child achieve the success that you want for her. There are certainly enough negative influences in our culture that teach kids not to value themselves. You can help to counteract those influences by showing the child that she is important, valued, and loved.

In a very symbolic, as well as a real way, you can send a message to a child that she's a shining star in your life. Now you can literally name a star after her. We found a service dedicated to doing just that. Read about it in the box on the next page.

International Star Registry

(www.starregistry.com)

For $48, plus shipping and handling, you can name a star after your child and have the star's name copyrighted. The child will then receive a certificate, dedication date, and telescopic coordinates of the star, plus a booklet with charts of constellations and a larger chart with the star circled in red.

A child will most likely be thrilled at the thought of having a star named after her. Other benefits are that it will encourage her to learn about stars and the universe in which we live. She may learn about different constellations of stars and galaxies. She can also read about our own galaxy, the Milky Way. The child will be astounded to discover how far away even the closest stars are. She may develop an interest in our own solar system and the comets and asteroids that pass in and out of Earth's orbit. And she may pay more attention to our space program and what scientists are doing when rockets and shuttles are launched into orbit. And most important of all, the child will feel connected to you each time she looks at the sky and searches for her star.

Give Things Related to Family History

Items that belonged to your parents or other family members may have special meaning to your children.

Items that have been owned and used in your family in previous generations could be more than merely forgotten things collecting dust in the attic. Instead they can be viewed as remnants of your family's legacy and its history, and thus serve a useful purpose in connecting your kids with the family's past.

First, try to get a sense of what would be of interest to your children. You might invite the kids to go through some old things in a chest in the garage under the pretext of "organizing" them. If a child shows special interest in something, make a mental note of it. Then when the next opportunity or occasion for a gift occurs, wrap up the item and give it to the child along with a card that reads, "Surprise!"

The very things that you may have forgotten for years might be items that your kids would greatly appreciate. Items of interest could include old comic books, dolls, stuffed animals, book collections (for example, Nancy Drew, Hardy Boys), model airplanes or cars, boxed games, or perhaps that special something that belonged to a relative favored by a child. Be the one to round up these things for your kids.

By giving the gift of a family heirloom from a deceased family member, such as Great Grandma's brooch, or Great Uncle Earl's pocket watch, you're helping to keep the memories of these special people alive. It's what they would have wanted you to do, just as you probably want your own things to be left to someone who appreciates them.

NANCY ONCE KNEW A NINE-YEAR-OLD BOY, *Alex, whose grandfather, Paw-Paw, had died unexpectedly. Alex had been very close to his grandfather, and the boy grieved this loss deeply. Alex's father often used a fishing pole and pocket knife which had once belonged to Paw-Paw. After Paw-Paw died, Alex's father decided that it was time to pass these items on to his son. He hoped this would help ease Alex's sense of loss. Alex was overjoyed and kept them displayed in his room. The two items reminded him of the times he had gone fishing with his grandfather and of the fun they had together. After that, Alex felt closer to his dad than he ever had since his parents' divorce.*

TIP 91 | Deliver Gourmet or Special Food Items

Delight your kid's taste buds with a specialty food item.

Many times, dads who initially lose emotional closeness with their children after a divorce are at a loss regarding how to reconnect with them. Using a sensory approach is a good way to overcome barriers to intimacy that may have built up. In addition to the methods already discussed, you may be able to reach your kids through their taste buds. You can figure out the best way to do this by finding out what their favorite foods are. What do your children like to eat? Most kids have a sweet tooth. Do they like chocolate? What about candy with nuts? What about nuts on their own?

Give your kids the unexpected surprise of a gourmet or unusual food item delivered to their house. Most likely, the type of food you send will have to be nonperishable and should be packaged well to prevent contamination. You may send it by regular mail, overnight mail, or Federal Express, depending on the type of food. Some retail stores will mail the food for you, or you may place an order online and have the item sent directly to your kids.

Check with your ex-wife first to make sure your choice of food is a wise one. Take into consideration if a child has a weight problem or if she wears braces. Has she had tooth cavities in the past from eating too many sweets and not taking care of her teeth? While you want to provide a treat for the children, keep in mind that the gift could go unappreciated if it can't be eaten because of a health concern.

8 Recommended Web Sites for Home Delivery

Here are some mouth-watering gourmet-candy web sites:

- www.candydirect.com
- www.enstrom.com
- www.kailua-candy.com
- www.shoemakers-candies.com

These web sites offer gourmet popcorn:

- www.popcornpalace.com
- www.popcornranch.com

Two web sites offering gourmet nuts are:

- www.gourmetnutsandcandy.com
- www.kremaproducts.com

TIP 92

Choose Sports Equipment

Encouraging an interest in sports can support your children both physically and socially.

One complaint that we often hear from parents is that their kids spend too much time either watching television or playing computer games. If these are your kid's major activities, you'll want to encourage them to exercise or participate in some sport so that their lifestyle is healthier and more balanced. Balance is about developing a range of attributes in your kids that will help them to be successful and happy as they grow into adulthood. You can encourage physical fitness in your kids by directing them towards sports activities, or better yet, you could set the example by keeping physically fit yourself.

At Christmas and birthdays give gifts that would help a child become involved in sports. First, check with a child to see what sports he prefers. Don't rely on what you liked as a kid. Perhaps you loved basketball, but your son shows little inclination toward that sport. He may instead have a passion for swimming. Try to help the child match his natural abilities and talents. Some sports require better hand-eye coordination or faster running speed.

Encouraging sports doesn't mean pushing a child into competitive athletics. The focus should be on promoting an enjoyment of physical exercise or of having the experience of belonging to a team. If a child wants to pursue competitive sports, you'll find out soon enough.

BRENDA'S DAD LOVED TO TAKE EVENING WALKS *after dinner. When her parents separated, he took an apartment in the same Seattle neighborhood where Brenda and her mom lived. Brenda became overjoyed when her dad started calling and asking if she would join him on his walks. Brenda's mom at first resisted letting the child go with her dad. But then he took Brenda to buy new walking shoes during one of her visits to see him. He also sent a nice note to Brenda's mother reminding her how important it was for Brenda to get exercise. Finally Brenda's mom decided the walks were going to be good for her daughter. Brenda and her dad became known around their neighborhood because of their strolls together in the evenings. These were the times when Brenda got to know her father best, when he would tell her stories of his boyhood. The experiences also got Brenda in the habit of walking in the evenings, which she still does today.*

TIP 93 | Bond with Shirts and Hats

By wearing similar clothing, you establish something in common with a child.

Buy the same shirt or cap for yourself in your own size that you buy for a child when you're together at a special time or place. Wear these clothing items at the same time and have someone else take a picture of the two of you. After the child returns home, pick out an attractive picture frame that can stand on a dresser or desk and mail the framed picture to the child.

The photograph will suggest that the two of you are alike and that you have something in common, namely the way you are dressed. Since we tend to like others who are like us, the child will get a reinforced message that subconsciously reminds him, "My dad likes me, I like him, and we're alike." If he sees this picture in his room every day, it will remind him of the bond that exists between you. Whenever you call him, it could make him more receptive and more willing to share with you what's going on in his life.

WHEN KENNY TOOK HIS DAUGHTER ANNE *white-water rafting, the rafting company took pictures of the raft as it went through the dramatic class IV falls. Kenny bought himself and Anne copies of one of the pictures. He also bought brightly colored shirts with the rafting company logo on them for himself and Anne. Later in the week, a neighbor made a picture of Anne and her dad wearing their matching shirts. After Anne returned home, Kenny put both pictures in a double frame and mailed them to her. Every time Anne looks at the pictures, she is reminded of the fun time she had with her dad and of the similarities between them. Anne continues to treasure her shirt and to think of her dad whenever she wears it.*

CHAPTER 11

Say "Thank You" Often: Express Gratitude to Others

A simple expression of gratitude can go a long way in creating a sense of goodwill among the people who have contact with your kids. Put yourself in their place. Wouldn't you be more likely to "go the extra mile" for a parent who takes the time to thank you for your contribution to his children's development? People appreciate having others acknowledge what they have contributed in terms of time, effort, and concern.

Your thanks can extend beyond the social sphere that your children exist in. Giving thanks to your ultimate spiritual reality can be effective in reminding you of the blessings in the lives of you and your kids. You may find that by giving thanks, you acquire a new attitude toward what occurs. You may also discover that the number of blessings in your life will increase over time as you continue to develop your feelings of gratitude.

Finally, your act of giving thanks provides an example to your kids of your approach to dealing with people and with life itself. As they encounter challenges in the years ahead, the children will benefit if you help them realize that one of the basic rules of success lies in gratitude. The person who focuses more on reasons to be grateful in life, rather than on reasons to complain, will move more readily toward success than the person who is fixated on everything that's wrong. And the person who gives thanks for the many things in life that are good is more likely to look at solutions rather than dwell on problems.

TIP 94 | Credit Your Ex-Wife and Her Family

Doing the most difficult thing often brings the greatest reward.

Since the children live with your ex-spouse, she clearly has the power to either help you or to sabotage your efforts to stay connected to the kids. It will ultimately benefit both you and your children if you can make an effort to put yourself in your ex-wife's shoes and see the situation from her point of view too. Being empathetic to her may be a challenge for you, but an ounce of empathy on your part could bring you a pound of gratitude from your ex in return.

Life for divorced mothers who have custody of their kids is definitely very stressful. More than likely, your ex has to work at a full-time job as well as being a mom to your children. She has financial pressures and time pressures. No doubt, you have pressures and stress in your own life, even without your children living with you full-time, so you can imagine what it must be like for her. If you can bring yourself to sincerely thank your ex for all that she does, she may be much more willing to help you maintain good relations with your kids.

At appropriate times, you might also mention to your ex-wife how much you appreciate what her parents, siblings, and other relatives do for your children. Be sure to express your gratitude directly to these family members yourself, as well. Saying "thank you" to all the family members who nurture your children shows that you're not taking them for granted. It also increases the likelihood that you can maintain a smooth, cordial relationship with them, for your children's sake. A thank you can be expressed by sending a card, a handwritten note, or an email message. Or pick up the phone and express your gratitude directly.

SAM HAD A MESSY DIVORCE FROM HIS WIFE. *For several years they were not on speaking terms. Naturally this affected his relationship with their daughter Jessica, who was only three months old when they divorced. When Jessica was about to enter the first grade, Sam realized that he wasn't as involved in her life as he wanted to be. When he tried to call Jessica between weekend visitations, he seldom was able to talk to her. He suspected that his wife checked the caller ID and ignored his calls. If she did answer, he was told that it wasn't a convenient time to talk to Jessica. After consulting with a counselor, Sam decided to bite the bullet and thank his ex for all that she had done by herself in raising their daughter. This did not have an immediate effect. However, over time, as he continued to express his appreciation, she began to soften a little. Finally his ex-wife started letting him speak to Jessica most of the time when he called.*

 TIP 95 **Praise Your Family Members and Friends**

By thanking those who are closest to you, you encourage them to continue helping your kids.

Is there anyone in your extended family who assists you with your children? Do you have neighbors, members of your church, or friends who go out of their way to be nice to your kids during visitations? Perhaps your sister routinely invites your children to play with her kids at their house or to spend the night. Maybe one of your neighbors is good about including your kids when planning activities for her children. Anytime you have gotten help from the people close to you in taking care of your children, it's important to say thank you. If those people know that you really appreciate what they did, they'll be more inclined to continue.

Grandparents are often sources of security and stability for children during the times of uncertainty following a divorce. How have your parents helped you with your kids since you separated from your ex-wife? What would they appreciate from you right now as a way of thanking them? Ask this question to yourself about everyone who has contributed to your kids' happiness, even in small ways. It only takes a few minutes to express appreciation to the people who are contributing love, support, and assistance to your children's lives. The best way to assure that your kids continue to receive nurturing is to thank the people who are providing it now.

AL HAD CUSTODY OF HIS EIGHT-YEAR-OLD SON *James during the month of July. During part of each day when Al had to work, James stayed at a nearby day care center. Al worried about having to leave James in day care for such long hours. He was greatly relieved when a neighbor offered to pick James up at three o'clock each day when she picked up her own son Henry. Afterwards the kids would play together at the neighbor's house. Sometimes Henry's mother would take the kids to the neighborhood public swimming pool until Al came home from work. Al found a way to thank Henry's mother; he took the two boys horseback riding one weekend. On the way back home from the horse stable, he stopped at a garden shop and bought a beautiful blooming plant. Al presented this to Henry's mother with a thank you card.*

TIP 96	**Recognize Your Child's Mentors**

As important role models, the instructors in your children's lives will do a better job if given the recognition they deserve.

There are a number of adults in your kids' life who are in a position to help them learn and grow up to be responsible adults. Besides your children's relatives, these people are usually the most influential adults to your kids. These mentors include school teachers, coaches, piano teachers, dance instructors, art instructors, karate teachers, Scout leaders, ministers, choir directors, and Sunday school teachers. It's important to take the time to express your gratitude for what they're contributing. You can express this by sending thank-you notes, but you could also occasionally send thoughtful gifts to the people who help your kids at school and elsewhere.

3 Tips For Thanking Mentors

1. **Write a thank-you note** in which you mention something positive and specific the mentor did for a child.

2. **Buy a small, inexpensive gift for the mentor,** and send it through the child. If possible, choose something that relates to the subject taught or an item that the mentor has indicated an interest in. Good times to send gifts are at Christmas, the end of the school year, birthdays (if known), or other special occasions.

3. **Say thank you verbally on a frequent basis,** taking the time to pause for a moment, make eye contact, and smile as you express your appreciation.

JASON HAD NOT PAID MUCH ATTENTION *to the teachers of his teenaged son Reid before the divorce. Jason's wife Holly had usually been the one to interact with Reid's instructors. After Jason and Holly separated, this father realized that he needed to become more involved. Jason spoke to his ex-wife about assuming more of the responsibility regarding contact with Reid's teachers and coach. After following through, he was impressed by how much most of the teachers really seemed to care about his son's progress. At the end of the school year, Jason sent thank-you cards to all of these contacts. During the next school year, Jason looked for opportunities to express his appreciation to the many professionals who were contributing to his son's development.*

TIP 97 | Thank Your Higher Power

The act of thanking your ultimate spiritual reality will give you a sense of serenity.

Giving thanks to your conception of a higher power is an age-old way to bring yourself the blessings of serenity and peace of mind. Make a list of all that you have to be thankful for. Don't forget the things you may have taken for granted, like your health, freedom, job, and kids.

You may even go so far as to thank God for the help and love that your ex-wife gives to your children. Your ex may never know that you do this, but it can help *you*. It could soften your stance toward your ex in a way that will indirectly cause her to reciprocate with concessions of her own. This turn of events can only help you and the children in your efforts to maintain a close bond.

WHEN JOEL FIRST GOT DIVORCED, *he was so angry that any talk of blessing or forgiving his ex-wife Carol only made him upset. Joel and his ex both felt pretty bitter. Each of them was pointing a finger at the other. What changed was that Joel had a near-death experience in a car accident. This experience influenced his perspective on what was important in his life. Joel began to be more grateful for the miracle of life and all that he had. The clincher came when his ex-wife got breast cancer. Joel became concerned for his son because he didn't want him to be without a mother, even though the relationship with her had been so rocky. Also, this was a woman he had spent twelve years with. He couldn't just ignore the life-threatening illness that she had. And, too, it made him even more aware of his own mortality, which he'd already been thinking about since the car crash. Shortly after Carol told Joel that she was sick, he found himself on his knees, praying that she would recover. To make a long story short, she finally did recover, after extensive treatment and surgery. Today Joel thanks God for all that he has, including an ex-spouse who is a good mother for his son.*

CHAPTER 12

Teach Values and Beliefs: Set the Example

Values are nothing more than our beliefs about what's important. Many people have only vague ideas about what they stand for. Consequently they can be swayed to behave in directions that are not in the best interests of themselves or their kids. The more aware you are of your own beliefs and values and of how you make important life decisions while still being true to yourself, the more successful you'll be in setting a helpful example for your kids.

How grounded are you in your beliefs? Do you have strong spiritual convictions or faith? Are you really sure that you even know what your core beliefs are? What things or qualities do you value in life? How do you rank the importance in your life of money, family, friends, education, honesty, career success, fun, a nice house, a fancy car, and adventure? How do you handle temptations to lie, be dishonest, or present a false picture of yourself? Are you willing to risk losing friends if they put pressure on you to do something that goes against your beliefs or values? How do you want your children to handle these types of decisions?

If you've clearly defined for yourself what you believe in and what values are important to you, your life is more likely to reflect these choices. Also, if you're really clear with the children about your own beliefs and values, it will help them to formulate what theirs are. When this happens, you are helping your children live with the integrity that comes when behavior is consistent with those beliefs and values.

The starting point is always to look at your own beliefs and values first and to use them as a compass in choosing which directions to go in your own life. A child quickly picks up on the difference between what a father says he believes in and the actual choices he makes. Actions carry more weight than words, and a child is constantly absorbing your beliefs and values by observing how you live your life. You are setting an example even when you don't realize what you're teaching at the moment.

> Your actions ultimately reveal the beliefs and values that you hold in your heart.

TIP 98 | Set an Example with Your Own Faith

If you let the children see what a difference your faith has made in your life, they will be more inclined to follow your example.

One of the effects of the terrorist attacks of September 11, 2001 is that people in our country have been taking stock of what's truly important to them. As a father, you set the example for your kids through your own behavior, attitudes, and beliefs. In each interaction with your children, you have the opportunity to show them in subtle ways what your spiritual beliefs are and whether they actually make a difference in how you choose to live.

By living with faith according to your most intimate values, you reside in the best possible space emotionally and spiritually to nurture a close, connected relationship with your children. Some fathers may attend church with their kids, pray before meals and bedtime, and read the Bible or other spiritual books. Other fathers might set an example by slowing down to have quiet contemplative moments, by taking time to be outdoors to appreciate the beauty of nature, or by remembering to express gratitude to a higher power. By setting the example with your own faith, you can empower your children with spiritual resources as well as strengthen your connections with each other.

DAVID HAD JUST ARRIVED FROM ROCHESTER *to attend a business meeting in Seattle when he heard the news of the September 11th World Trade Center disasters. He immediately called his teenaged daughter Melinda on her cell phone, reaching the girl at the boarding school she attends in Upstate New York. Through the anguish of the next several days until he could get a flight back to New York, David stayed on the phone frequently with his daughter. Although they had not been close since her mother and David had divorced five years before, he found himself sharing the spiritual beliefs with her that had helped him weather tough times. Together on the phone they cried and even prayed for the victims and their families. Their bonding through this terrible ordeal was one of the best things that ever happened to them. As a result, David and his daughter made plans to attend one of the memorial church services when he returned. Since then, the two have started attending church together when they can, and David and Melinda are continuing to talk about issues such as faith, evil, death, and their concepts of God. This has brought them closer, and this closeness is something good that came out of the September 11th experience.*

| TIP 99 | ## Show Your Values by Your Actions |

A father who does not stand for something is teaching his kids to fall for anything.

You show your kids what you believe is important by your behavior. You may say that you love your children, but your actions will tell the real story. How well your talk is matched by how you act is a measure of your integrity and commitment to living by your values.

If you value helping your kids to feel emotionally secure, you'll want to show your love and support for them through your acts of kindness, financial support, and your efforts to be there when they need you. You will follow through on promises, and you'll make every effort to be consistent and reliable. When you say you'll call on Thursday night to arrange for your Saturday visitation, you'll make calling on time a top priority. Through your actions, your children learn whether or not they can trust and believe you.

Nancy has seen many disappointed, hurt, and angry kids in counseling sessions after their fathers have made promises they did not keep. The children might have been told they would spend the weekend with their dad, who then never showed up and didn't even call. The kids were devastated, and the message they received was that their father doesn't value them or really care about their feelings. After a few experiences of unkept promises, kids learn that what dad says is very different from what he actually does.

RAYMOND SAID HE LOVED HIS TWO CHILDREN, *but his behavior gave a mixed message. On some occasions, he would lavish them with expensive gifts that he could scarcely afford. Yet, on other visitation dates, he would fail to show up for scheduled visits and would sometimes go for weeks without even calling them. When they were younger, Raymond's kids would get excited when he promised to take them swimming or to the circus. But when so many promises and plans didn't materialize, they "shut down" emotionally when their dad talked about all he was going to do for them. They had learned through experience that their dad was "all talk."*

TIP 100 | Do Volunteer Work Together

When you set the example by giving back some of the blessings you have received, you send a powerful message to your kids.

Everyone receives good fortune in some measure, and everyone has reasons to be thankful. If you have your health, family members and friends who care about you, a roof over your head, and food to eat, then you have blessings to be thankful for. While we're fortunate to live in a free country with many opportunities, there are still numerous individuals and good causes needing your help. You may choose to demonstrate your gratitude for your personal blessings by offering to assist with a worthy cause sponsored by your church, service club, community organization, or local government.

Doing volunteer work shows your kids that you take action when you believe strongly in a cause. It also demonstrates that you want to be a part of the solution and do what you can to help. For some individuals, giving to those less fortunate than they are is a way of showing compassion and sharing God's love. For others, giving embodies the spiritual belief that how they treat others is important because "What goes around comes around." Whatever your personal beliefs and reasons are, doing volunteer work with your children when they visit is a way to communicate what kinds of things are important to you.

Most children like to help others and to see how their actions are making a difference. Sharing an experience of doing volunteer work together can help you to connect in a special way with your kids.

WHEN AMY VISITED HER FATHER DURING SUMMER *vacation, he surprised her with a question. Amy's dad wanted to know how she would feel about going with him one day each week to help serve lunch at a local soup kitchen. He prepared Amy for the experience by telling her about the homeless shelter, some of the heartwarming stories he had heard, and how various church groups had become involved. While Amy was somewhat apprehensive at first, her dad reassured her that he would be right beside her the whole time. Amy was surprised at how much she enjoyed the experience. She was also surprised to see this side of her father. Amy had never seen him do anything like this before, and she listened intently when he explained why he felt community service was important. After Amy returned home, she regularly asked her father during their phone conversations about certain people she had met at the soup kitchen and about how things were going there.*

TIP 101 | Meditate/Pray/Worship Together

By looking for opportunities to share your spiritual beliefs, practices, and experiences, you're giving your kids a powerful resource for coping with life.

Most of the world's religions teach the power of believing in an essence, energy, or intelligence that is much larger than human understanding can comprehend. Some call this essence God, while others may use the terms Divine Love, Great Spirit, or Higher Power. You get to choose how you define it to your children.

You can show your children through your example that by tapping into that inner source of strength, you can do more in the outer world. Teach your kids your approach for tapping into that power. If you believe in prayer, show the children how you pray and how you listen for guidance. Take advantage of opportunities to worship together, either in a church setting or informally. If you meditate, share with the children how you meditate quietly when you want to still your mind. Or if you find your greatest sense of spiritual connection when you are outdoors in nature, find ways to share these experiences with your kids.

Be an example through your consistency in practicing the spiritual principles of your faith. Strengthen the cords of your spiritual connection to your children and enrich your relationship.

BEN AND HIS DAUGHTER LORI WERE SWINGING *in Ben's patio hammock while gazing in awe at the radiant summer night sky. They had been talking about what it means to feel the presence of God. Ben had wanted to share with Lori how his understanding of a spiritual presence in life had grown in the years since the divorce from her mother. Yet Ben had momentarily been at a loss for words to explain how the experience had really been for him. Suddenly a falling star shot across the night sky. A few seconds later, another followed. Ben turned to Lori and said, "You see, sometimes God sends signals that I have to pay attention to. That is when I have the strength to make important decisions and to take action, such as now. This is one way that I have come to experience God in my life." The two silently watched the sky for a few minutes, enjoying their feelings of connectedness with each other and with the surrounding universe.*

❖ ❖ ❖

We'd Like Your Help

PLEASE ASSIST US IN WRITING the next Staying Connected™ Series book.

If you are a divorced dad and have used any methods that we have not mentioned to stay bonded with your kids, we'd love to hear from you. Please write up your experiences and send them to us. Or you might know what another father is doing that could be helpful for other dads to know about. If so, please contact us. We need your help.

Mothers and other family members are also invited to share effective methods that they have seen divorced fathers use to stay closely connected with their children. Ex-husbands, brothers, sons, and nephews could be sources for effective bonding tips and inspirational stories.

Please share your story or method with us so that others may benefit. If you're the source of a tip that is used in our next book, we'll credit you within its pages with permission.

Whenever you help another, you help yourself as well. We're looking forward to hearing from you!

You may reach us at **www.staydad.com**. Or by snail mail at:

Adesso Press
P.O. Box 489
Pinson, AL 35126

Additional Resources

Books

Ashley, Steven. *Fathers Are Forever: A Co-Parenting Guide for the 21ˢᵗ Century*. Columbus, Georgia: Brentwood Press, 2001.

Braver, Sanford L., Ph.D., with O'Connell, Diane (contributor). *Divorced Dads: Shattering the Myths*. New York: J.P. Tarcher, 1998.

Bryan, Mark A. *The Prodigal Father: Reuniting Fathers and Their Children*. New York: Three Rivers Press, 1998.

Condrell, Kenneth N., Ph.D., with Small, Linda Lee (contributor). *Be a Great Divorced Dad*. New York: St. Martin's Press, 1998.

Klatte, William C. *Live-Away Dads: Staying a Part of Your Children's Lives When They Aren't a Part of Your Home*. New York: Penguin, 1999.

Knox, David, Ph.D., with Leggett, Kermit (contributor). *The Divorced Dad's Survival Book: How to Stay Connected with Your Kids*. New York: Perseus Books, 1998.

McClure, F. Daniel; Saffer, Jerry B. *Wednesday Evenings and Every Other Weekend: From Divorced Dad to Competent Co-Parent. A Guide For the Noncustodial Father.* The Van Doren Company, 2000.

Prengel, Serge. *Twelve Steps for the Divorced Dad.* Mission Creative Energy, 1998.

Prengel, Serge. *Still a Dad: The Divorced Father's Journey.* Mission Creative Energy, 1999.

Ricci, Isolina, Ph.D. *Mom's House, Dad's House: Making Two Homes for Your Child.* New York: Simon & Schuster, 1997.

Thayer, Elizabeth, Ph.D. and Zimmerson, Jeffrey, Ph.D. *The Co-Parenting Survival Guide: Letting Go of Conflict after a Difficult Divorce.* Oakland, CA: New Harbinger Publications, Inc., 2001.

Web Sites

http://www.dadsvoices.com/
This site provides divorce support for men. Stepmothers, second wives, and girlfriends are also welcome here.

http://www.divorcedfathers.com/
This site is dedicated to assisting fathers in parenting issues and helping them through a support group network.

http://gocrc.com/
This is the site of the Children's Rights council, which works to strengthen families through education. Their motto is: "The best parent is both parents."

http://www.acfc.org/
This is the site of the American Coalition for Fathers and Children, which promotes equal rights and reform for all parties affected by divorce.

http://www.parent.net/
This is the site of Parent News, which offers information on a variety of parenting topics, as well as a free e-mail newsletter.

http://www.saafamilies.org/
This is the site of the Stepfamily Association of American, a national, nonprofit organization dedicated to successful stepfamily living.

Index

"We believe in the power of love and persistence to transform relationships. We also believe that even small changes a father makes can have major impact on the rapport with his children."
— Nancy Wasson and
Lee Hefner

About the Authors

NANCY J. WASSON, PH.D., is a Licensed Professional Counselor with more than two decades of experience in working with children, parents, and families. In addition to her M.Ed. in Counseling and Ph.D. in Educational Psychology, she is a National Certified Counselor and a Certified Clinical Mental Health Counselor. In her many years of service as a former school counselor and school psychologist, Nancy encountered numerous children whose lives were impacted by divorce. She is currently in private practice and works in counseling with children of divorced parents, seeing firsthand what their needs, fears, and concerns are. Nancy also counsels divorced parents who want to know what they can do to stay closely connected with their children. Nancy has a strong personal interest in divorce parenting issues, as she herself is a divorced mother.

LEE HEFNER is the noncustodial father of a teenaged daughter. For almost a decade, Lee has searched for ways, like so many other divorced fathers, to connect more deeply with his child. Lee's candid appraisal and extensive experience of what has worked results from interviews with other divorced parents as well as his own personal story of sorrow, struggle, triumph, and joy. With a background as a consultant in the aerospace field, Lee found himself unprepared for the task of maintaining a long-distance emotional link with his daughter. It was only after taking responsibility for achieving the outcome he desired and developing some of the methods and approaches in this book that Lee was able to improve the mutual feeling of connection between himself and his child.

The Staying Connected™ Series published by Adesso Press is dedicated to helping people connect more deeply with their loved ones.

Give the Gift of

Divorced Dads:
101 Ways to Stay Connected with Your Kids

to a Dad or a Mom

Check Your Local Bookstore or Order Here

____ YES, I want _____ copies of *Divorced Dads: 101 Ways to Stay Connected with Your Kids* for $14.95 each.

Include $4 shipping and handling for one book, and $2 for each additional book. Alabama residents must include sales tax of 5%.

Canadian orders must be accompanied by a postal money order in US funds.

Paym   for
deliv

My c

Pleas

Nam

Orga

Addr

City/

Phor

Ema

Card

Exp.

Sign

Fax

Senc

Tele

Web

Ema

Post

3512